Dining with Sherlock Holmes

A Baker Street Cookbook

Dining with Sherlock Holmes

A Baker Street Cookbook

by Julia Carlson Rosenblatt
and Frederic H. Sonnenschmidt

THE BOBBS-MERRILL COMPANY, INC.
Indianapolis/New York

Published by the Bobbs-Merrill Company, Inc.
Indianapolis   New York

Designed by Ingrid Beckman
Manufactured in the United States of America

First printing

Library of Congress Cataloging in Publication Data
Main entry under title:
Dining with Sherlock Holmes.
    1. Cookery, English. 2. Menus. I. Rosenblatt, Julia C.
TX717.D56   641.5'941   76–11610
ISBN 0–672–52194–6

Contents

Foreword

It all began at Reichenbach Falls in Switzerland, in a scene reminiscent of that described by Samuel Rosenberg when he recounted the birth of his book *Naked Is the Best Disguise*.[1] My husband and I, beset by heavy fog during a ski vacation, were motoring through the countryside in search of a break in the haze. Holmes, Watson, and Baker Street couldn't have been further from our thoughts. Suddenly, we came to the village of Meiringen; the car jolted to a stop; my head nearly hit the windshield, and my husband, who had been driving, pointed excitedly to a road sign: REICHENBACH FALLS. "Reichenbach Falls!" There, with the car still stopped in the middle of the road, he recounted the epic tale of Sherlock Holmes's mortal struggle with the evil Professor Moriarty. That incident ignited the spark of Sherlockian fervour. We were never to be the same again.

One night, late in 1972, my husband and I were seated on either side of a cheery fire at our home in Pleasant Valley. How wonderful it would be, we thought, to have a gourmet meal such as Holmes and Watson might have had in 1895. There was only one place in the country that could do it: The Culinary Institute of America in Hyde Park, New York (affectionately known as the C.I.A.). The idea became reality on June 2, 1973, when more than 100 Sherlock Holmes enthusiasts enjoyed a grand Sherlockian repast, prepared under the direction of Chefs Frederic Sonnenschmidt, Bruno Ellmer, Steven Beno, and George Metropolis. The casual remark, "There ought to be a cookbook . . . ," led to the partnership of professional chef and Holmesian aficionado that produced the present volume.

I owe a special word of thanks to the members of my family. Daughter Betsy curbed her two-and-one-half-year-old curiosity to the extent of leav-

---

[1] Indianapolis: Bobbs-Merrill, 1974.

ing my typewriter and notes intact. My parents, Anabel and Harold Carlson, stepped in whenever help was needed. But most of all, my thanks are to my husband, Albert M. Rosenblatt, who was in on this project from its very beginning, and who was my assistant in every way possible. It is to Albert M. Rosenblatt, holder of the Baker Street Irregulars' titular investiture of "Inspector Bradstreet," that I wish to dedicate my portion of this work.

JULIA C. ROSENBLATT
Pleasant Valley, New York
January 1976

Acknowledgements

Many people were generous with their knowledge, their ideas, their libraries, whenever they had an opportunity: Susan Dorler, Glenn Laxton, John Linsenmeyer, Michael Murphy, Donald Novorsky, Michael Whelan, and Dr. Julian Wolff. A special word of thanks is owed to John Bennett Shaw, who shared many items from his copious collection to get us started on the straight path of research, and to Peter Blau, Jon Lellenberg, and Jennifer Van Tuyl, who read portions of this manuscript and helped materially with suggestions.

We are grateful to Chefs Noble Masi, Bruno Ellmer, and Willie Spry for their generous assistance; and to Jacob Rosenthal, President Emeritus; and Henry Ogden Barbour, President, of the Culinary Institute of America for their kind encouragement.

We would be ungrateful indeed were we not to acknowledge a debt of gratitude to Sir Arthur Conan Doyle, without whom the deeds of Holmes and Watson would be forever entombed in a certain dispatch box. Also to other late, lamented authors like Vincent Starrett, Edgar Smith, Christopher Morley, and William S. Baring-Gould, whose works are a continuing source of inspiration.

This book could not have been written but for the many hours during which we were allowed to explore the stacks of the Vassar College Library and the Confrerie de Chevalier des Taste Vin Library at the Culinary Institute of America.

Some of these recipes were tested in the pristine kitchens of the Culinary Institute of America; some of them in the Rosenblatt home kitchen; and some in the kitchens of our adventuresome friends. The most enjoyable testing and tasting session was at the First Annual Bring-Your-Own-

Sherlock Holmes Covered Dish Christmas Feast of The Hudson Valley Sciontists, hosted graciously by Mr. and Mrs. John Alden of Staatsburg, New York.

Thanks also to Laura DeMarco for her monumental effort in typing this manuscript.

JULIA C. ROSENBLATT
FREDERIC H. SONNENSCHMIDT
Pleasant Valley, New York
January 1976

☞

Dining with Sherlock Holmes

A Baker Street Cookbook

☞

The Gastronomic Holmes
and the Cuisine
of His England

In aeons to come, the archaeologist of the future will sift through the libraries of our crumbled civilization and will undoubtedly come upon the commanding presence of Sherlock Holmes and Dr. John H. Watson. Perhaps he will study Watson's memoirs and the countless scholarly treatises and biographies which followed.[1] He will then begin to understand Holmes's personality and to accord him his rightful place in our history. Then, he will turn to an encyclopaedia, only to be told, "Sherlock Holmes is a popular hero of English Detective fiction."

We offer nothing to enlighten the confused archaeologist, but we hope that he and others of his era will still appreciate a good roast beef, plum pudding, or English trifle. We invite him to transport himself to the Baker Street digs of Holmes and Watson, where, with the contemporary reader, he will sit near a cheery fire at Mrs. Hudson's table. Furthermore, we assure the scientist of the future that whether or not the exploits of the Baker Street sleuth were lived only in fiction, Holmes and his dauntless chronicler are very real parts of our civilization.

To the devotees of Sherlock Holmes, the 56 short stories and 4 novels published under the authorship of Sir Arthur Conan Doyle are the Canon, or the Sacred Writings. Tongue-in-cheek or otherwise, critics from

---

[1] Of the 60 tales, 56 are in the first person of Watson; 2 are in the words of Holmes himself; and 2 are in the third person.

all walks of life have written volumes about the experiences and habits of the Great Detective of Baker Street. The literature of the field, known as the Writings on the Writings, or the Higher Criticism, has spawned endless discourse over the most minute details of Holmes's life and "death."

We have chosen to write about a Sherlock Holmes and a Dr. Watson who are more than mere creations of fiction. We can visualize Holmes in his various poses—a tireless sleuth, hot upon a scent; a Baker Street companion, dazzling Watson with his "mind-reading"; or, even today, a retired centenarian, quietly keeping his bees upon the South Downs of Sussex. The late Vincent Starrett, a beloved Sherlockian author, has expressed the feeling and the certainty with these words: ". . . they still live for all that love them well: in a romantic chamber of the heart, in a nostalgic country of the mind, where it is always 1895."[2]

Sherlock Holmes does not enjoy a reputation as a gourmet. Much about the Great Detective, including his gastronomic expertise, went unreported. Like Watson, who mistakenly concluded that Holmes was without relatives because he never mentioned his family,[3] we risk falling into the error of believing that Holmes's knowledge of gastronomy was nil because he reportedly seldom mentioned food. The few morsels given us indicate that Holmes was, indeed, a true gourmet. It was he who ordered an "epicurean cold supper" consisting of "a couple of brace of woodcock, a pheasant, and a *pâté de fois gras* pie with a group of ancient and cobwebby bottles."[4] It was Sherlock Holmes who provided that "oysters and a brace of grouse, with something a little choice in white wines" be ready for a dinner with Dr. Watson and Detective Athelney Jones.[5] Furthermore, he recognized, although even a non-gourmet may perceive it as well, that "chloroform vapour does not help the palate."[6]

True it is that "his diet was usually of the sparest, and his habits were simple to the verge of austerity."[7] He took great pride in his willingness to eschew comfort. "A loaf of bread and a clean collar. What does a man want more?" boasted Holmes in *The Hound of the Baskervilles*, when he camped secretly in a primitive neolithic hut on Dartmoor. Watson, however, noted that Holmes was not as ascetic as his boast, for he "had con-

[2] Vincent Starrett, *The Private Life of Sherlock Holmes,* Chicago: The University of Chicago Press, 1960, p. 62.

[3] "The Greek Interpreter."

[4] "The Adventure of the Noble Bachelor." Which reminds us that Doyle wrote of Sherlock Holmes, ". . . I feel towards him as I do towards *pâté de fois gras,* of which I once ate too much, so that the name of it gives me a sickly feeling to this day." (Reported in Hesketh Pearson, *Conan Doyle,* New York: Walker & Co., 1961, p. 133.)

[5] *The Sign of Four.*

[6] "His Last Bow."

[7] "The Yellow Face."

trived, with that catlike love of personal cleanliness which was one of his characteristics, that his chin should be as smooth and his linen as perfect as if he were in Baker Street." Furthermore, the variety of tins, empty and otherwise, in that rude hut revealed a diet rather more varied than bread alone. A man who can live and dine well under Spartan circumstances is indeed an epicure.

Even Holmes's occasional denial of food adds to the evidence that the Detective was a gourmet. He seldom ate while working intensively on a problem. When he did take time out for a meal, all discussion of an unsettling nature was strictly banned until the table was cleared. If the case was too pressing to allow a respite, then dining had to wait until he could relax. Holmes was so consistent in this regard that the comparatively slow-witted Watson could deduce the progress of a case thereby: "The mere sight of his excellent appetite was an assurance of success."[8]

If Holmes, the gastronome, is misunderstood, so is his native cuisine. The poor reputation of English food is not entirely justified. English cuisine was essentially simple home fare, relying on the quality of the ingredients for its excellence.

To compare English cooking with French *haute cuisine* is a little like comparing the folktale with the classical novel. Each has a different origin, and can be compared validly only within its own genre. The most distinctive English dishes were created in the kitchen of the home or country inn. They were created to match the economy and daily schedule of the home cook or innkeeper's wife. The ingredients came naturally: whatever was available.

It is no wonder, therefore, that the most distinctive English main dishes are concoctions of meat, vegetables, herbs, and spices, cooked together. Some are served hot from the pot; others baked into a pie. Whatever the form, these blends will be recognized as stews. Anyone who looks down upon the stew as lowly poor man's food is certain to spurn English cooking, no matter how well prepared it is.

Another distinctive English culinary creation is the suet pudding. It is a combination of flour, breadcrumbs, suet, sugar, and eggs, plus as many other ingredients as availability and inventiveness will allow. This doughy mixture must be poached for hours before serving. The result is a heavy but tasty dish, which, although it lacks the dainty elegance of most continental delicacies, can be excellent indeed. It is represented in this book by the traditional Christmas plum pudding, which, curiously but characteristically, contains no plums.

This is not to imply that classical cuisine was not a part of English life. In fact, the cuisine of the late Victorian and Edwardian eras is most remembered in the lavish dinner party. Luncheons and dinners of ten to

8 *The Valley of Fear.*

twelve courses, often bearing French names, were not uncommon. The appetite of the affluent was immense, and their gastronomic pretensions were even greater. Many of the more impecunious social aspirants served more dishes than they expected their guests to eat, having instructed the servants to whisk certain serving platters away from the table before anyone had touched them so that they could be served at the next night's dinner party.

Unsurpassed for lavishness, of course, were the dinners served by the royal court. Almost legendary is the poultry construction consisting of a turkey stuffed with a chicken, in turn stuffed with a pheasant, in turn stuffed with a woodcock, and so on down to the tiny, bite-sized ortolan.[9] Everywhere the monarch went, a lavish display of food followed. It must be noted, however, that a hungry diner fared far better during the reign of King Edward VII than he did during that of Queen Victoria, for no one was allowed to eat after the monarch had finished dining. The Queen's dainty appetite sometimes meant that, in spite of the ever-flowing food, the guest departed hungry. King Edward's appetite was more fully appropriate to the grandeur of the table.

But it is not at the lavish party that we find Holmes and Watson. Holmes spoke of an invitation to one as "one of those unwelcome social summonses which call upon a man either to be bored or to lie."[10] In the country, the setting for many an elaborate house party, Holmes referred scornfully to "the usual overfed, underworked staff of a large English country-house."[11] We ordinarily find Holmes and Watson at home or in a country inn, dining on local food, obtained as fresh as possible and cooked without a great deal of continental pretense.

In spite of the excellence of distinctively English cuisine, we are forced to admit that were the contemporary diner to be placed in a time machine and transported back to an epoch even so recent as the past century, he would find the food, for the most part, quite unpalatable. When refrigeration was rare, and the germ theory of illness undreamed of, the preparation and handling of food lacked some of the care that we today take for granted. Of course, not all precautions were lacking. Bacterial action may not have been a known villain, but diners were well aware of bad-tasting food and gastric upset, and care was taken to avoid both. We do not doubt, however, that many a case of food poisoning was passed off as mere indigestion. Furthermore, we must regretfully acknowledge that some of the Victorian's favourite dishes taste bad to the modern American palate; for example, over-aged game.

[9] The birds were boned before being rolled together. In today's terms we can imagine it to be like an exotic turkey roll with layers of different colours and flavours of meat.

[10] "The Adventure of the Noble Bachelor."

[11] "The Adventure of Wisteria Lodge."

Throughout this book, wherever we have perceived a conflict, we have taken license with authenticity in favour of taste and ease of preparation. After all, when we yearn for the world of Sherlock Holmes, it is for the snug, gas-lit security of the age, not for its discomforts. We long to sally forth with Holmes and Watson amidst the swirls of yellow London fog without inhaling its sulphurous fumes. So it must be with the food. We have tried to limit the ingredients to things obtainable in the typical supermarket, to use American measurements,[12] and to employ "every modern improvement which the march of civilization demands."[13]

Holmes and Watson did not suffer from the lack of convenience in the old-fashioned kitchen. All of that was under the able control of their dedicated landlady, Mrs. Hudson, who kept house for them, catered to their eccentricities, and had their meals ready for them whenever they were pleased to dine. Unpredictable mealtimes, as perplexing as they may be to the modern cook, were a constant challenge to Mrs. Hudson. The kitchen in the nether reaches of 221B Baker Street did not easily yield up an impromptu repast. When Holmes breakfasted at 7:00 A.M., Mrs. Hudson arose at 5:00. If yeast bread or rolls were contemplated, she first assembled the dough and set it aside to rise.

Then she set about to light the kitchen fire. She brushed the range, cleaned the hearth, adjusted all the dampers and flues, laid a bed of cinders at the bottom of the grate, and, placing a layer of crumpled paper on the cinders, topped it off with a cover of kindling wood. Alternate layers of coal and wood were added before Mrs. Hudson ignited the paper, which set up a blaze. As soon as the wood and coal caught fire, she readjusted the draughts and dampers, and went about the rest of the morning's work.

Gas stoves were known in London while Holmes and Mrs. Hudson were yet at Baker Street, but we doubt that she went to the trouble and expense of renovating the kitchen, even after Holmes's payments had become "princely." After all, she had become accustomed to the routine. Compact oil stoves could be had for convenience, but they had the unfortunate habit of exploding, and we doubt that Holmes would have allowed such a dangerous contraption in the house.

The fire having begun, Mrs. Hudson rinsed the kettle and filled it with fresh water to boil. The stove would not be heated sufficiently to cook for some time, but meanwhile there was plenty to do. She had to get the breakfast room ready, sweep and wipe the hall and the stairs, shake out the hall mats, and in general give the house a neat, comfortable appearance before the business of the day commenced. It would not do to be sweeping the stairs when Inspector Lestrade arrived.

---

[12] For a discourse on weights and measures, see the chapter entitled "Elementary, My Dear Watson."

[13] Sherlock Holmes in "The Adventure of Charles Augustus Milverton."

Finally the hour would come when either Holmes or Watson would ring the bell for breakfast. Often it was Holmes who arose first, but Mrs. Hudson knew that Watson was less than tolerant if his rising was not anticipated in time, too.

After the breakfast debris was cleared, Mrs. Hudson could busy herself answering the door for Holmes's callers (or for Watson's, if he had any) and tending to her own business with tradesmen. Whatever else she had to do, she would soon have to make lunch and consider dinner preparations. We do not doubt that frequently when Holmes was absorbed in an investigation, he advised Mrs. Hudson not to plan dinner. It would have been unkind not to warn her that the fruits of her afternoon's labours would go untasted, and Watson could always dine at his club. Holmes's thoughtfulness in this matter may be why, on at least two occasions, it was he who was responsible for the evening meal at Baker Street.

Canonical mealtimes followed no set pattern. That is to say that they were irregular. Although little is revealed about what Holmes and Watson ate while on a case, much is known about *when* they ate, for Watson had a habit of marking the passage of time by reference to mealtimes. We can visualize Watson, who once was visibly irritated that his breakfast place was not set in time,[14] attending greatly to the regularity of his meals, but little to what was on the plate. Holmes was the epicure, Watson merely his dining companion.

Thanks to the monumental work of the Sherlockian gastronome John Bennett Shaw, who counted every specific mention of a meal or item of food in the Canon,[15] we can confidently say that not only did Holmes and Watson have their three meals a day, they had, on the average, more than three meals per story. The phrase "three meals a day" refers to contemporary American practice. During the age of Holmes and Watson, English meals and mealtimes were undergoing transition, so that the Victorian diner could choose to partake of any or all of the following repasts: breakfast, morning tea, luncheon, afternoon tea, high tea, dinner, or supper.

Similarly, a luncheon or dinner could consist of any (but for the middle class not all) of about a dozen courses. They were not completely standardized, but they might include the following: hors d'oeuvre, soup, fish, entrées, meats and vegetables, punch or sherbet (to refresh the palate), game, salad, sweets, savoury, cheese, fruit, coffee or tea. Of these, the most foreign to contemporary American custom is the practice of eating a savoury (a spicy or piquant tidbit) after the sweets.

---

[14] He showed this "unreasonable petulance," as he called it, in *A Study in Scarlet.*

[15] John Bennett Shaw, "Alimentary, My Dear Watson," *Baker Street Journal,* 1967, *17*, pp. 98–100. He counted 198 specific references to a meal or specific item of food (or 3.30 per story!), and 108 to drink other than water.

We understand, with this wealth of material before us, the difficulty that Watson had when he selected which of the cases to set before the public. We have endeavoured, insofar as possible, to select those which illustrate some interesting feature of the lives of Holmes and Watson and of the fare they ate.

We invite the reader, therefore, to follow the example of Holmes and to put aside the cares and worries of the present. Enter a more tranquil world, and dine heartily. Should the reader, perchance, eat too much, "The doctor has a prescription containing hot water and a lemon which is good medicine on a night like this."[16]

[16] "The Adventure of the Golden Pince-Nez."

"Elementary, My Dear Watson"

Mrs. Hudson's Biscuits
1½ cups flour
1 teaspoon butter
1 teaspoon baking powder
½ teaspoon salt
¾ cup milk

1) Mix the baking powder,
   salt and flour together.
2) Rub the butter with your
   fingers.
3) Add the milk and beat until
   the mixture becomes soft dough.

4) Grease a baking pan.
5) For each biscuit's spoon out
   a level teaspoon of dough,
   and drop it on to pan, having
   each biscuit 1 inch apart.
6) Bake them in 350-400° oven
   for 6-10 minutes. They will
   keep for one week in a
   tin canister.

FLOUR

Salt

Beans

COCAIN

Vineg

NUTMEG
ALLSPICE

"It has been my habit to hide none of my methods from . . . anyone who might take an intelligent interest in them."

—Sherlock Holmes in "The Reigate Squires"

Elementary it is: The starting point of any culinary adventure is the measurement of ingredients. At precisely this point, in the United States at least, the professional chef and amateur cook part company. The professional carefully weighs his ingredients. Most American amateurs, surrounded by an array of measuring cups and spoons, ladle out the ingredients by volume. In this book, we have bowed to custom and have given the amounts in volume, except for items for which the weight can be inferred without a home scale (e.g., items that are bought by weight). Because this book is written essentially for an American readership, and because one should not seek lightly to alter the habits of others, we give in to the facts as they are, recalling the words of Sherlock Holmes: "I can discover facts, Watson, but I cannot change them."[1]

Measuring ingredients by weight rather than volume is concededly more precise. A cup of flour on the average weighs one-fourth of a pound. It will be heavier or lighter depending upon how the cup is filled.[2] A

[1] "The Problem of Thor Bridge."

[2] Recall that "Individuals vary, but percentages remain constant." (Sherlock Holmes in *The Sign of Four*.)

session with a cup, a scale, and a sack of flour will, upon successive weighings, prove instructive, although somewhat messy.

Sifted flour is lighter than unsifted. The recipes in this book presume that the flour is unsifted when it is measured, even though it may be sifted later as part of the recipe's method. In Holmes's day, however, it was not advisable to use unsifted flour under any circumstances. It was bought in large quantities and kept in larders which were not entirely impervious to insect or rodent invaders. The "criminal relics" that turned up in the Baker Street butter dish[3] were nothing compared to what might be baked in the pie if Mrs. Hudson did not first sift the flour.

Regrettably, the English language has adopted the same word, "ounce," to refer to both volume and weight measurement. Should 8 ounces of shortening be squeezed into a measuring cup or placed on a scale? For some substances, like shortening (including butter and lard), water, and granulated white sugar, it does not matter much. That is, 16 fluid ounces (1 American pint) of water weighs 16 ounces (1 pound). For other substances, however, measuring the unintended quality will spell disaster. Flour, for example, is approximately half as heavy as water, and therefore an 8-ounce cup of flour weighs only about 4 ounces.

To further compound matters, the American volume measures are not identical to the English measures of the same name. The English cup or half pint consists of 10 fluid ounces, whereas the American is 8 ounces. Throughout this book, we have used American Standard measures. To reduce confusion, we offer the following table of equivalents:

> 1 quart = 4 cups = 32 oz.
> 1 fifth (*e.g.,* one wine bottle) = 1/5 gal. = 25.6 oz.
> 1 pint = 2 cups = 16 oz.
> 1 cup = ½ pint = 8 oz.
> 3 tbsp. = 1 large jigger = 1½ oz.
> 2 tbsp. = 1 small jigger = 1 oz.
> 1 tbsp. = 3 tsp. = ½ oz.

To Sherlock Holmes, it was "an axiom . . . that the little things are infinitely the most important."[4] When it comes to cooking, he would have to agree that seasoning is one of the crucial little things. English cooks of Holmes's day made good use of herbs and spices. Every little garden had its array of herbs which were used fresh in season, and dried carefully for use when not. In addition, tropical spices were imported from the length and breadth of the Empire, upon which the sun never set.

The English liked to flavour meat with herbs from the animal's habitat. And in a similar matter of subtle flavour, they preferred to construct

---

[3] As described in "The Musgrave Ritual."
[4] "A Case of Identity."

meat pies from dough that used the fat of the corresponding animal. Hence pork lard was the shortening in pork pies, beef drippings in beef pies, and so forth. Because animal fat is not usually kept for long in the typical American household, we have specified vegetable shortening in dough recipes, but we suggest adding the charm of variety to meat pies by substituting the same amount of animal fat for the shortening when it is possible.

The cardinal rule for any seasoning is moderation. It is always easier to add a touch more of something than it is to redeem a dish that has been given an overdose of flavour. One-fourth to one-half teaspoon of any dried herb is usually about right for a four-portion dish. Because fresh herbs are usually about half the strength of dried ones, it is generally safe to double this amount when fresh herbs are available. Remember, also, to cut the amount in half when dried herbs are substituted for fresh. Strong tropical spices are more safely limited to about $\frac{1}{8}$ teaspoon for a four-portion dish unless the diner's taste buds emphatically demand more.

In some recipes, we have used that time-honoured model of imprecise measurement, the "pinch."[5] This may be defined as the amount that a person will pick up between thumb and forefinger. Naturally, a large-fingered man is likely to add twice as much seasoning as a small-fingered woman, and so we have used the word "pinch" only when this amount of variation may be tolerated. In recipes for which something minute but more precise is indicated, we have used a measure that is gaining increasing popularity among chefs, the "knife tip."[6] A knife tip of something is an amount that just covers the tip of a knife. Standardization is assured; whether a knife is large or small, the very tip will be the same as that of any other knife.

As to salt, we heartily recommend the use of coarse cooking salt,[7] also known as Kosher salt, in all of these recipes. Fine table salt contains iodine and other additives. We have no quarrel with iodine, which is beneficial to health, but iodine may be added to the diet in other ways. Table salt contains other chemicals to make it pour well in damp weather. Some gourmets are sensitive to it, and at best the chemicals do nothing to enhance the flavour of the cooking. It is better to keep table salt on the table and coarse salt in the kitchen.

In most recipes, the amount of salt is given as a range, or modified by the words "or to taste." This is because individual tastes vary greatly.

---

[5] Holmes himself would have used this imprecise measure, according to his acquaintance young Stamford, if he were to test the effect of a vegetable alkaloid on himself or another (*A Study in Scarlet*).

[6] The knife tip, of course, has long been popular among the criminal classes.

[7] Coarse cooking salt is not to be confused with coarse rock salt, which was used to pack a certain cardboard box in a Sherlockian adventure of that name. Rock salt could be used for food, but it should be ground in a pepper mill first.

Furthermore, in a display of stubborn Yankee independence, many Americans salt their food at the table no matter how it has been seasoned in the kitchen. For this reason, many a chef in the United States deliberately undersalts the food, hoping that in partnership with the diner he will achieve the correct seasoning. Most European chefs expect to season the food to perfection themselves without any later intervention.

Frequently, when a recipe calls for pepper, we have stated the amount in terms of the number of grinds on a pepper mill. We have done this because freshly ground pepper is far better than ready-ground, and because the grind is a relatively precise way to express a small amount. One grind is approximately equal to one pinch.

Vanilla sugar may be unfamiliar to some readers. It is available in packages, or it can be made at home by putting a vanilla bean into a jar of sugar and keeping it there. The sugar will absorb the vanilla flavour from the bean. In recipes calling for vanilla sugar, it is possible to substitute 2 teaspoons of plain sugar and 2 to 3 drops of vanilla extract for each 2 teaspoons, or standard-sized package, of vanilla sugar.

Many recipes in this book call for grated orange or lemon peel. The rinds of oranges or lemons are usually chemically treated before they are sent to market. We recommend dipping them very briefly in a boiling solution of 2 parts water and 1 part vinegar before grating them. The boiling vinegar solution does not smell very good, and your fellow lodgers may object as Watson did to some of Holmes's efforts "which involved much heating of retorts and distilling of vapours, ending at last in a smell which fairly drove [Watson] out of the apartment."[8] Your companions, however, will forgive you when they taste the result.

Perfection in seasoning depends, not only on good choice and caution, but also on how and when the cook tastes the food. When tasting a salad dressing, sample it after adding everything but the oil. Do not add the oil until it has been seasoned to satisfaction. When tasting something hot, put a small portion into a small saucer, and slurp it into your mouth. The extra intake of air will mix with the food, enhancing the tasting, and helping to prevent a burnt tongue.

One final word of advice: It is not only important to measure ingredients carefully, it is also important to follow the method of the recipe precisely. Observe the marination times. Follow every step as closely as possible. The manner in which the ingredients are combined and cooked may be as important as the ingredients themselves (sometimes more important). We leave you with the words of Sherlock Holmes: "They say that genius is an infinite capacity for taking pains. It's a very bad definition, but it does apply . . ."[9]

---

[8] *The Sign of Four.*
[9] *A Study in Scarlet.*

Breakfast at Baker Street

We join Mr. Sherlock Holmes and John H. Watson, M.D., at breakfast in the sitting room of their lodgings at Baker Street. Outside, swirls of London fog enshroud the cobblestoned byways so familiar to the detective and his companion. A fire in the grate dispels the early-morning chill. Mrs. Hudson, their ever-faithful housekeeper, brings in the morning meal.

Breakfast is, by far, the most prominent meal in the Sherlockian Canon. An eminent authority on things Holmesian and on things gustatory, John Bennett Shaw, has counted 73 specific mentions of breakfast, as opposed to 30 references to lunch, 3 to high tea, and 58 to dinner or supper.[1]

The hours at which breakfast was served can be described only as irregular, if the meal was eaten at all. Usually, if we can take Dr. Watson's accounts as representative, late breakfasts were typical. Mr. Holmes was "a late riser as a rule,"[2] that is, he was "usually very late in the mornings, save upon those not infrequent occasions when he stayed up all night."[3] Watson, too, admittedly enjoyed the habit of sleeping late. In "The Boscombe Valley Mystery" we find him, married and a busy practitioner, yet lingering at the breakfast table at 10:45. Late breakfasts were not universal, however, for in "The Adventure of the Engineer's Thumb" Wat-

[1] In "Alimentary, My Dear Watson," *Baker Street Journal*, 1967, *17*, pp. 98–100.
[2] "The Adventure of the Speckled Band."
[3] *The Hound of the Baskervilles.*

son was not surprised to find Holmes prepared to breakfast shortly after 7:00 A.M. Breakfast followed a practice which would rather defeat the appetite of most of us: ". . . smoking his before-breakfast pipe, which was composed of all of the plugs and dottles left from his smokes of the day before, all carefully dried and collected on the corner of the mantelpiece." To add to our vicarious gustatory uneasiness, on that particular morning, Holmes was confronted with a bleeding hand from which the thumb had been recently severed. The stout-hearted Mr. Holmes "ordered fresh rashers and eggs," and prepared to join Dr. Watson and the unfortunate victim in a "hearty meal."

We should like to have said that Sherlock Holmes recognized the virtues of arming himself nutritionally before sallying forth in quest of his targets. But, alas, it was not always so. Moreover, we can scarcely ascribe Holmes's early-morning strength to breakfast power. It will be remembered that the brute Roylott of "The Speckled Band" visited Baker Street before Holmes and Watson had partaken of even a morsel of food. Nevertheless, after Roylott bent a steel poker with his bare hands, Holmes bent it back and then sat down to the day's first meal. Mrs. Hudson was ready to await the conclusion of such impromptu adventures before bringing in the repast. She was also uncomplainingly patient when, on another occasion, Holmes spurned an already-prepared breakfast: "At present I cannot spare energy and nerve force for digestion."[4] Dr. Watson enjoyed the meal with gusto.

The unpredictable habits of her lodgers forced the ever accommodating Mrs. Hudson to grow quite flexible in her meal preparation. On mornings of particular haste, she sent them on their way with simple but nourishing fare: eggs, toast and jam, and coffee. Elementary. In "The Adventure of the Retired Colourman," Watson reported observing eggshells and toast crumbs as evidence that Holmes had breakfasted before him.

The breakfast egg was an important constituent of the Victorian breakfast. Whatever else was served, a bowl of eggs in the shell commonly rested on the sideboard for morning nourishment. This simple, quick dish requires great care. To this day, chefs hotly debate the precise procedure to produce the perfect egg. We fancy that Mrs. Hudson was very adept at bringing the eggs to just the proper consistency, for we know that Mrs. Hudson's lodgers were not heedless of the quality of their breakfast egg. Sherlock Holmes once remarked to Watson that "even so trivial a matter as cooking an egg demands an attention which is conscious of the passage of time." The reader will be relieved to know that Mrs. Hudson was not responsible for the overcooked eggs that inspired the Master's critical comment in "The Problem of Thor Bridge." A new cook was on

[4] "The Adventure of the Norwood Builder."

duty that morning, one whose attention was drawn away from the preparation of breakfast, as Holmes deduced, to the "love romance" in the *Family Herald.*

The Stanley Hopkins Breakfast

Mrs. Hudson's best-timed breakfast efforts were occasionally thwarted when adventure was at hand. On one morning in particular, Sherlock Holmes and Dr. Watson had just completed an investigation. The case had taken them away from Baker Street to Woodman's Lee, to solve the murder of seafarer Peter Carey, otherwise known as "Black Peter."[5] Having returned to their comfortable lodgings, the pair had invited Detective Stanley Hopkins to join them for breakfast. Mrs. Hudson had prepared an "excellent breakfast" for 9:30 A.M. The detective arrived on time, but the meal was delayed until the three prospective diners had interviewed and handcuffed the murderer of the sea captain.

"I must really apologize, Hopkins," said Sherlock Holmes. "I fear that the scrambled eggs are cold. However, you will enjoy the rest of your breakfast all the better, will you not, for the thought that you have brought your case to a triumphant conclusion." Sherlock Holmes was correct to apologize, for scrambled eggs may not be successfully reheated.

The breakfast menu follows:

> Broiled Grapefruit with Ginger
> Scrambled Eggs with Broiled Mushrooms and Ham
> Oatcakes
> Orange Marmalade
> Coffee

[5] "The Adventure of Black Peter."

☞ Broiled Grapefruit with Ginger

Grapefruit
1 tablespoon brown sugar for each grapefruit half
⅓ to ½ teaspoon ginger powder for each grapefruit half
1 teaspoon honey for each grapefruit half

Cut the grapefruit in half, and section it. Mix the sugar with the ginger powder and sprinkle over the fruit. Drizzle 1 teaspoon of honey over each half and broil for 2 to 3 minutes until brown.

☞ Scrambled Eggs with Broiled Mushrooms and Ham

Scrambled eggs
Large white button mushrooms
Ham

1) Prepare the scrambled eggs.[6]

2) Trim the roots from the large white button mushrooms. Wash them, place them on a buttered tray, and broil them for 3 to 4 minutes.

3) Cut the ham into slices, and broil it for 2 to 4 minutes.

4) Set the ham on a plate, and top it with the scrambled eggs and broiled mushrooms.

[6] With respect to the scrambled eggs, we offer a couple of helpful hints. In order to keep them soft and creamy, use gentle heat, stir them constantly, and add a little cream (1 teaspoon for each 3 eggs) just as the eggs are almost set but a little underdone. This will stop the cooking and add moisture to the eggs. Also, do not season the eggs before they are cooked. They do not always need added salt. This reminds us of what the late Monsignor Ronald Knox had called "Sherlockismus," the most famous of which is the incident of the dog in the nighttime, from "Silver Blaze":

Inspector: Is there any other point to which you would wish to draw my attention?
Holmes: To the curious incident of the dog in the nighttime.
Inspector: The dog did nothing in the nighttime.
Holmes: That was the curious incident.

Accordingly, we imagine Holmes and Watson, having just settled into their lodgings at Baker Street, discussing Mrs. Hudson's cuisine:

Holmes: We can rely on Mrs. Hudson to cook scrambled eggs to perfection. I observed how she used the seasoning before cooking the eggs.
Watson: But she added no seasoning.
Holmes: That is how I knew the eggs would be right.

☞ Oatcakes

Makes 8 oatcakes

1 ¾ cups regular oatmeal
¼ teaspoon baking powder
½ teaspoon salt
1 tablespoon melted butter
5 to 8 teaspoons hot water

1) Pulverize 1 cup of the oatmeal in a blender, ½ cup at a time.

2) Combine the pulverized oatmeal, baking powder, and salt in a bowl, and stir in the melted butter.

3) When all the butter is absorbed, add the hot water, 1 teaspoon at a time, stirring constantly to make a firm dough.

4) Mould the mixture into a ball. Place it on a board, and sprinkle it with ¼ cup of oatmeal.

5) Roll the ball in the oatmeal until it is covered with it.

6) Spread another ¼ cup of oatmeal over the board. Roll the ball out into an 8-inch-diameter circle, approximately ⅛ inch thick.

7) Cut the circle into 8 pie-shaped wedges with a pastry wheel or sharp knife.

8) Scatter the remaining ¼ cup of oatmeal on a baking sheet and transfer the wedges to the sheet with a large spatula.

9) Bake the cakes for 15 minutes. When the wedges are light brown, turn off the heat and open the door of the oven.

10) Leave the oatcakes in the oven for 4 to 5 minutes more, or until they become firm and crisp. Serve them right away.

☞ Orange Marmalade

Oranges (any oranges may be used, but we recommend a proportion
    of 1 to 2 bitter oranges to 5 sweet oranges)
Sugar (13 ounces sugar for each pound of fruit)[7]
Water (½ cup water for each pound of fruit)

1) Wash the oranges thoroughly.

2) Remove the yellow peel from the oranges with a potato peeler. Cut the peel into very fine strips and set them in cold water. Bring them to a boil and drain them. Repeat this process twice.

---

[7] It will be necessary to weigh the fruit after peeling to determine the proper proportions.

3) Remove the white part from the oranges and cut the fruit into thin slices. Remove the seeds and the tough center post.

4) Bring the sugar and water to a boil. Add the fruit and the strips of peel, and boil the mixture until it is ready to jell. Test it by putting a small amount of the boiling liquid in a saucer and placing it in the refrigerator. If it is ready, the sample will soon jell. The boiling will take approximately 30 minutes. Stir frequently to prevent the fruit from sticking to the bottom and burning.

5) Pour the marmalade into sterilized jars and seal them.

Breakfast to Celebrate the Recovery of a Lost Document

Sherlock Holmes had said of Mrs. Hudson: "Her cuisine is a little limited, but she has as good an idea of breakfast as a Scotchwoman."[1] Most critics, responding to the word "limited," take this as a comment on the gracious landlady's culinary shortcomings; whereas Holmes meant this phrase as a very high compliment indeed. Said Samuel Johnson in 1773, "If an epicure could remove by a wish, in quest of sensual gratifications, wherever he had supped, he would breakfast in Scotland."[2] The implication of limitations was one of Holmes's customary jestful misstatements.[3] We can infer that this particular morning's feast was most praiseworthy and inventive. It was the breakfast at the conclusion of "The Naval Treaty." In this meal, Mrs. Hudson's most famous breakfast, she showed herself more than capable of producing the hearty morning repast for which the England of Holmes's time was so famous. Curried chicken with ham and eggs joined other tasty dishes to tempt the appetite of the breakfasters. Everyone was hungry, except Holmes's client, the unfortunate Percy

[1] "The Naval Treaty."
[2] Samuel Johnson, *Journey to the Western Islands of Scotland*, London: 1775, p. 124.
[3] As when, for example, Holmes referred to Watson's "native shrewdness," "innate cunning," and "Machiavellian intellect" in *The Valley of Fear*.

Phelps, whose lack of appetite was from worry over the loss of the document which had formed the basis of this adventure. None of Mrs. Hudson's tasty dishes could themselves satisfy the distraught clerk, but when Holmes produced the lost treaty from under one of the covers at the table, all was well again.

Peaches and Cream
Ham and Eggs
Chicken Corma
Rice with Raisins
Tea, Coffee

☞ Ham and Eggs

Serves 4

2 English muffins, cut in half and toasted
12 slices canned ham
12 asparagus tips (if possible, white)
4 teaspoons finely grated Cheddar cheese
½ cup Hollandaise sauce

1) Toast the muffins to a golden brown.
2) Roll up each asparagus tip in a slice of ham.
3) Sprinkle ½ teaspoon of Cheddar cheese over each muffin. Top each with 3 ham rolls and pour 1 ounce of egg sauce (Hollandaise sauce)[4] over each one. Sprinkle with the rest of the cheese.
4) Brown them under the broiler.

☞ Hollandaise Sauce

Makes ½ cup

2 egg yolks
1 teaspoon cold water
¼ to ½ cup melted butter
¼ to ½ teaspoon lemon juice, or to taste
A pinch of salt

[4] Where are the eggs? the diner may ask. In the Hollandaise sauce, of course!

1) Combine the egg yolks and water in the top of a double boiler and beat them with a wire whisk over hot (not boiling) water until they are fluffy.

2) Add a few spoonfuls of butter to the mixture and beat it continually. Add the rest of the butter slowly until the sauce starts to thicken, and then add the lemon juice. If there is any butter left, continue to whip it into the sauce. Take care that the water in the bottom of the double boiler never boils. Add the salt, and for lighter texture, beat in a tablespoon of hot water, if desired.

☞ **Chicken Corma**

Serves 4

    1 roasting chicken (2 pounds), cut into pieces
    1 medium-sized onion
    ¼ pound butter
    ½ teaspoon mashed garlic
    ½ teaspoon ground saffron or turmeric
    1 teaspoon ground coriander seeds
    ½ teaspoon ground chili
    2 cups water
    15 ounces plain yogurt[5]
    ½ teaspoon salt, or to taste
    1-inch piece of ginger, sliced
    ½ teaspoon each of cloves, black pepper, cumin seeds

1) Slice the onion finely. Brown the onion and the garlic in butter, then place in a small dish and set aside, leaving the fat in the pan.

2) Put the ground spices into a cup of water. Add them to the fat in the pan. Cook them for 3 minutes, stirring occasionally.

3) Add the chicken pieces; mix them well. Simmer them covered for 20 minutes. After 20 minutes, remove the cover and continue the cooking.

4) After the liquid has evaporated, continue to cook the chicken until it is brown.

5) Crush the browned onions. Add them to the chicken along with the yogurt, the salt, and the remaining spices. Add a cup of water, and simmer until the chicken is tender.

---

[5] Yogurt was not widely known in the cuisine of Holmes's London. Mrs. Hudson used buttermilk, but we recommend yogurt as producing a better result.

☞ Rice with Raisins

Serves 4 to 6

2 tablespoons butter or margarine
1 cup uncooked rice
2 cups stock or water
½ red onion studded with 2 cloves
3 ribs of celery
1 carrot, cut in half lengthwise
2 to 3 tablespoons raisins
Salt to taste (begin with 1 teaspoon)

1) Heat the butter. Add the rice, and stir it for 1 to 2 minutes over low heat until it is glossy.

2) Add the stock or water, the onion pique (onion pierced with cloves), celery, carrot, raisins, and salt. Mix them well and bring them to a boil.

3) Finish the cooking by placing the rice, covered, in a preheated 400°F. oven for 20 minutes.

4) Remove it from the oven and take out the onion, celery, and carrot. Stir it well to allow the steam to escape. Adjust the seasoning and serve.

Note: The celery, carrot, and onion (cloves removed) may be diced, sautéed in a little butter, sprinkled with parsley, and served as a vegetable at the same or a subsequent meal.

Marksman's Breakfast

Among Mrs. Hudson's special menus, we fancy, was one that was inspired by the indoor target practice of Mr. Sherlock Holmes. This practice did not please Watson, and it could hardly have delighted Mrs. Hudson. To quote Watson: "I have always held . . . that pistol practice should distinctly be an open-air pasttime; and when Holmes in one of his queer humours would sit in an arm-chair, with his hair-trigger and a hundred Boxer cartridges, and proceed to adorn the opposite wall with a patriotic

V.R. done in bullet pocks, I felt strongly that neither the atmosphere nor the appearance of our room was improved by it."[1] The devotion of Mrs. Hudson to her eccentric boarder was made clear by her tolerance of this practice and in many other ways: She showed desperate concern over Holmes's health in "The Adventure of the Dying Detective." She maintained the quarters at 221B Baker Street unchanged for three years while all the world (save for Mycroft Holmes and the villain Colonel Sebastian Moran) thought Holmes to be dead. At the risk of her own life, she manipulated the wax bust of Holmes so that it might serve as a worthy target for the murderous Colonel Moran in "The Adventure of the Empty House." Most Holmesian scholars believe that Mrs. Hudson left London with Holmes to keep house for him in his retirement to Sussex, and that in 1914, during "His Last Bow," Holmes for the first recorded time referred to her by her Christian name, Martha.

> Eggs with Gunpowder Butter
> Potato Pancakes
> Apple Sauce
> Sweet Rolls
> Coffee, Milk

☞ Eggs with Gunpowder Butter

Serves 4

8 fried eggs
5 tablespoons butter
4 teaspoons sherry

1) Remove the eggs from the pan to a hot platter.
2) Place the butter in a pan and heat until it is brown but not burnt.
3) Add the sherry (be prepared for flame)[2] and pour it over the eggs.

---

[1] This is only one of the eccentricities described by Watson in "The Musgrave Ritual," and referred to again in "The Adventure of the Dying Detective."

[2] This combination of ingredients is suggested for its gastronomic effect, but its incendiary effect might well be included in *The Whole Art of Detection*, Sherlock Holmes's planned *magnum opus*. It will be remembered that Holmes used a fire alarm in "A Scandal in Bohemia" to pry from Irene Adler the secret hiding place of an important photograph. As he observed, "When a woman thinks that her house is on fire, her instinct is at once to rush to the thing which she values most. . . . A married woman grabs at her baby—an unmarried one reaches for her jewel box."

☞ Potato Pancakes

Serves 6 to 7

7 to 8 medium-sized raw potatoes (2 pounds)
1 cup milk
1 to 2 teaspoons salt, or to taste
1/3 teaspoon nutmeg
1 teaspoon parsley
2 eggs
1 1/2 tablespoons cornstarch
Fat (butter, oil, or lard)

1) Peel the potatoes and grate them.

2) Pour them into a cheesecloth and press them well to remove all the water from them.

3) Add all of the above ingredients except the fat to the dry potatoes and mix them well.

4) Heat the fat in a pan and drop the potato mixture, 1 tablespoon at a time, into the fat. Brown them well on either side.

☞ Apple Sauce

Serves 6 to 7

6 to 7 medium-sized apples (2 pounds)
1 cup water
A pinch of cinnamon or lemon peel
2 heaping tablespoons sugar

1) Wash the apples well, and cut them into quarters without peeling them. Remove the cores.

2) Cook them in the water with the cinnamon or lemon peel until they are soft.

3) Puree them in a blender or through a food mill. Add the sugar and cool.

☞ Sweet Rolls

Makes 3 1/2 dozen rolls

1 package dry yeast
1/2 cup lukewarm milk

½ cup light brown sugar
1 cup sweet butter
2 large eggs, beaten
6 cups sifted flour
1½ teaspoons salt
1 cup sour cream (at room temperature)
Chopped nuts
Brown sugar

1) Dissolve the yeast in the lukewarm milk.

2) Cream the sugar and butter together until the mixture is smooth.

3) Beat the eggs until they are light.

4) Combine 4½ cups of sifted flour with the salt.

5) Combine the yeast, the sugar-butter mixture, the eggs, and all but 3 tablespoons of the sour cream (which *must* be at room temperature).

6) Stir them into the 4½ cups of flour. Beat for 3 to 4 minutes with a hard rubber spatula. Cover the bowl with a towel, and refrigerate the dough for 2 hours.

7) After the 2-hour rest period, remove the dough from the refrigerator and let it stand until it doubles in bulk.

8) Punch it down, and add the rest of the sifted flour, or as much of it as is necessary to make a light, spongy dough.

9) Beat it for 2 minutes.

10) Divide the dough into 2 or 3 parts, and roll each into an oblong. Spread the oblongs with the remaining sour cream; sprinkle them with finely chopped nuts and brown sugar, and roll them lengthwise like a jelly roll. Cut each roll into 1-inch slices and put them, cut side down, on a greased pan to rise until they are double in size.

11) Bake them at 375°F. for 20 to 30 minutes, or until they are golden.

The Sign of Four

At no time was breakfast more welcome to Holmes than after he had been up all night sleuthing. "It was no uncommon thing for him to be away for days and nights on end when he was hot on a scent."[1] Occasionally, but not often, Watson joined him on an all-night chase. During *The Sign of Four*, both of them were away literally tracking a scent. A suspect had stepped in some creosote, and with the aid of a mongrel named Toby, the Detective and his Boswell followed the track for miles, becoming only momentarily sidetracked when the trail of the culprit crossed that of a creosote barrel. The true scent led to the river's edge, and having discovered all that they could there, Holmes suggested the next course of action: "Take this hansom, drive home, have some breakfast and get an hour's sleep. It is quite on the cards that we may be afoot to-night again."

Watson reported, "A bath at Baker Street and a complete change of clothes freshened me up wonderfully. When I came down[2] to our room I found the breakfast laid and Holmes pouring out the coffee." Remarked Holmes, ". . . you have had enough of the case. Better have your ham and eggs first." By inferring that Watson had tired of the mystery, however, Holmes was wrong, for Watson confessed, "If Holmes could work to find the criminals, I had a tenfold stronger reason to urge me on. . . ." The reason, we know, was that the search was, at least in part, taken in the interests of Miss Mary Morstan, who was eventually to become Mrs. Watson.

> Melon with White Wine
> Ham and Eggs Wensleydale
> Kedgeree
> Scones
> Coffee

☞ Melon with White Wine

Serves 4 to 6

  1 ripe melon (cantaloupe, honeydew, Persian, etc.)
  3 to 5 tablespoons sugar
  Juice of 1 lemon
  1 cup white wine (dry or sweet), or less

1) Peel and seed the melon. Cut it into 2- to 3-inch slices.
2) Put a layer of melon slices in a glass dish, and sprinkle the slices with

---

1 "The Adventure of the Beryl Coronet." This is one of the many metaphors in which Watson likened Holmes to a hound.

2 Watson often mentions descending to breakfast, leading to the inescapable conclusion that his bedroom was upstairs from the sitting room. It is generally accepted that Holmes slept in a room adjacent to the sitting room.

some of the sugar and lemon juice. Add another layer of melon, and repeat the process until all the melon is used.

3) Pour the wine over the melon. Do not use too much wine, or the dish will be soupy. Chill it for at least 1 hour or overnight.

☞ Ham and Eggs Wensleydale[3]

Serves 4 to 6

6 to 8 eggs
3 ounces butter
1 cup sliced fresh mushrooms or ⅔ cup canned mushrooms
4 to 6 ounces canned ham, cut into *julienne* strips
4 to 6 ounces Wensleydale cheese, diced
Salt, if necessary
5 to 6 grinds of pepper
2 teaspoons chopped chives or 4 teaspoons chopped scallions

1) Break the eggs into a cup and stir them lightly.

2) Heat ½ ounce of butter and sauté the mushrooms for 2 to 3 minutes and set them aside.

3) Heat another ½ ounce of butter and sauté the *julienne* ham. Keep it warm.

4) Heat the remaining butter. Add the eggs, and stir them with a fork. Just before they begin to thicken, add the mushrooms and diced cheese. Stir them well and season them with salt and pepper.

5) Arrange the eggs in the center of a platter and surround them with the *julienne* ham. Sprinkle with chopped chives and serve with toast.

☞ Kedgeree

Serves 4 to 6

½ cup rice
1 pound smoked haddock[4]

---

[3] We are indebted to Sherlockian Jon Lellenberg for discovering this recipe. Holmes's biographer, the late William Baring-Gould, disclosed that the Great Detective was born in the North Riding of Yorkshire (*Sherlock Holmes of Baker Street,* New York: Clarkson N. Potter, 1962). Wensleydale is in the North Riding of Yorkshire, and it is safe to say that this was one of Holmes's favourite breakfast dishes.

[4] Smoked haddock is especially good, but ready-cooked or leftover fish may be used instead (in which case, of course, omit the second step in the recipe).

Water and milk to cover fish
3 hard-boiled eggs
1 tablespoon chopped parsley
1 tablespoon melted butter
1 teaspoon madras curry powder

1) Cook the rice according to the directions on the package.

2) Poach the fish in half water and half milk: Heat the mixture in a large kettle just to a boil, add the fish, and simmer for approximately 7 minutes.

3) Chop the eggs and mix with the parsley.

4) Flake the fish, then combine it with the rice, melted butter, curry, and half of the egg mixture. Heat and toss together. Place in a fireproof serving dish.

5) Sprinkle the remaining egg-and-parsley mixture over the fish.

6) Heat it in the oven for a few minutes before serving.

☞ Scones

Approximately 8 scones

2 cups flour
2 teaspoons baking powder
1 ½ teaspoons sugar
½ teaspoon salt
2 tablespoons shortening
1 egg
¼ to ½ cup milk

1) Mix together the dry ingredients and the shortening.

2) Rub in the flour with your fingertips until the mixture looks like coarse meal.

3) Beat the egg until it froths, and set 1 tablespoon of it aside in a small dish. Beat the milk into the remainder of the egg and pour it over the flour mixture. Use just enough milk to make a soft dough.

4) Mix together until the dough can be gathered into a compact ball.

5) Dust the dough lightly with flour, and roll it out on a lightly floured surface to a thickness of ¾ inch. Cut it into triangles or 2-inch rounds. Re-roll the scraps and cut them until all the dough is used.

6) Place the scones about 1 inch apart on a greased baking sheet and brush the tops lightly with the reserved beaten egg.

7) Bake them in the middle of a hot (400°F.) oven for 15 minutes or until they are light brown. Serve them immediately.

Note: The scones may be baked on a lightly greased griddle instead of in the oven.

Cold Beef from the Sideboard

A hearty English breakfast commonly included a meat dish or two, something which would be equally at home on the luncheon or supper table. In "The Adventure of the Beryl Coronet," it will be recalled, a cold joint of beef reposed on the sideboard from which Holmes cut a piece for a sandwich to take with him on a sleuthing expedition. It follows that on the subsequent morning, part of that roast appeared on the breakfast table in the form of a perennial English favourite, bubble and squeak.

This was the breakfast to which Watson descended to find Sherlock Holmes "with a cup of coffee in one hand and the paper in the other, as fresh and trim as possible." According to Watson's accounts, coffee was Holmes's favourite breakfast beverage. We should not err by concluding that Holmes never drank tea, however. He did on several occasions, including this very adventure, but it was always coffee for breakfast. In his Sussex retirement an "early cup of tea" had become a habit, perhaps replacing coffee as a morning drink. Both coffee and tea were sufficiently a part of Holmes's routine that when Watson described him as a "self-poisoner by cocaine and tobacco,"[1] he might have added caffeine to the list.

"You will excuse my beginning [breakfast] without you, Watson," apologized Holmes. Watson, of course, excused him, for this state of affairs had not been unusual. At least in the earliest days of their friendship, Watson observed that Holmes "had invariably breakfasted and gone out before I rose in the morning."[2] We do not know at what stage of their

---

[1] "The Five Orange Pips."
[2] *A Study in Scarlet.*

association it was that Holmes solved the problem of the Beryl Coronet, but by that time they most probably had adopted the practice of frequently breakfasting together.[3]

Holmes had breakfasted early to meet his client and unravel the entire mystery, bringing both joy and sorrow to the troubled man.

> Bubble and Squeak with Brown Sauce
> Pumpernickel Bread
> Coffee

☞ Bubble and Squeak

Serves 4 to 6

1 head cabbage
A couple of dashes of Worcestershire sauce
2 ounces butter
½ cup (about 3 ounces) diced onions
1 garlic clove
1 pound chopped beef or lamb[4]
½ teaspoon salt
⅓ teaspoon pepper
4 tablespoons breadcrumbs
½ pound bacon

1) Boil the cabbage in salted water until it is soft (about ½ to ¾ hour). Chop it coarsely, and salt it lightly. Season it with Worcestershire sauce.

2) Heat the butter, and sauté the onions and garlic. Add the chopped meat and sauté it for 10 minutes. Season it with salt and pepper.

3) Butter a fireproof casserole dish. Layer the bottom with cabbage.

---

[3] We may assume, because of Holmes's apology, that their breakfast habits had changed, but Watson did not give the date of this adventure. It began on a Friday, ". . . a bright, crisp February morning, and the snow of the day before still lay deep upon the ground, shimmering brightly in the wintery sun." It had to have been before 1892, the date of the story's first publication. William S. Baring-Gould has inferred by comparing the weather archives with other events in Holmes's career that the year could only have been 1890 (*The Annotated Sherlock Holmes,* New York: Clarkson N. Potter, 1967, Vol. II, p. 282), but in 1890 Watson was married and not living at Baker Street. This is indeed a mystery.

[4] Of course, on this particular morning, Mrs. Hudson made the bubble and squeak with already-cooked beef, the beef which had been on the sideboard the previous day, and from which Holmes had made a sandwich (see p. 34) .

Top it with some of the meat mixture, and sprinkle it with some of the breadcrumbs. Add another layer of cabbage, then a layer of meat and breadcrumbs. Continue the process, ending with a layer of cabbage. Top the whole with bacon slices, and bake it in a 350°F. oven for 30 to 40 minutes. Turn it out onto a tray, and serve it like a cake. Serve it with Brown Sauce (see recipe, p. 159).

☞ Pumpernickel Bread

*Makes one large loaf
or two small loaves*

1½ cups water
⅔ cup cornmeal
¾ cup molasses
1 tablespoon butter
1 tablespoon salt
2 teaspoons sugar
1½ teaspoons caraway seed, pounded slightly
½ square unsweetened chocolate
1 package yeast
¼ cup warm water (105°–115°F.)
1 cup mashed potato (prepared from instant)
3 cups rye flour
1 cup whole wheat flour, approximately
1 egg white mixed with 1 tablespoon cold water

1) Combine the water and ½ cup cornmeal in a medium-sized saucepan, and cook the mixture, stirring with a wooden spoon until it is thickened.

2) Remove it from the heat and add the molasses, butter, salt, sugar, caraway seed and chocolate. Stir until it is well blended, and pour it into a large mixing bowl. Set aside until it has cooled to warm (105°–115°F).

3) Meanwhile, dissolve the yeast in the ¼ cup water at 105°–115°F.

4) Add the yeast and potato to the mixture in the bowl. Blend it well and stir in the rye flour and 1 cup whole wheat flour. The dough will be stiff and sticky.

5) Turn the dough onto a work surface liberally sprinkled with whole wheat flour. Put a little vegetable shortening or oil on your fingers and hands before you start to knead. Keep the surface of the dough powdered with flour. Have a scraper handy to remove the gummy film of dough that accumulates on the work surface. Be patient; presently the dough will re-

spond and begin to clear the work surface, and your fingers. Knead it until it is elastic, though stiff.

6) Place the dough in a greased bowl, cover it with plastic wrap, and put it in a warm place (80°–85°). The dough will seem so heavy you may wonder how it could possibly rise, but it will. Let it rise until it doubles in bulk.

7) Punch down the dough, knead out the air bubbles for 30 seconds, and form the dough into a round, smooth ball. It may be divided into half and formed into two smaller loaves if you wish.

8) Dust the baking sheet with the rest of the cornmeal, and place the loaves on it.

9) Cover the loaves with waxed paper and return to the warm draught-free place until they have again doubled in bulk.

10) Preheat oven to 375°F. Brush the loaves with egg white blended with 1 teaspoon water and place in the oven. Bake for about 50 minutes.

11) Remove the bread from the oven. Tap the bottom crust. If it yields a hard and hollow sound, the bread is done. If not, return the loaves to the oven for an additional 10 minutes. If the loaves appear to be browning too quickly, cover them with a piece of foil or brown paper.

12) Remove bread from the oven and place it on a metal rack to cool. The bread will keep for several weeks, wrapped in foil or plastic.

Baskerville Breakfast

The Hound of the Baskervilles opened at the breakfast table. Dr. Watson was examining a walking stick left by an unidentified visitor. Sherlock Holmes was seated at the breakfast table with his back toward Watson:

"Well, Watson, what do you make of it?"

"How did you know what I was doing? I believe you have eyes in the back of your head," exclaimed the amazed Watson.

"I have, at least, a well-polished, silver-plated coffeepot in front of me," replied the Detective.

The visitor, whose walking stick provided a lesson in elementary deduction, was soon to reappear at 221B Baker Street. He was one James

Mortimer of Devonshire, who urgently unfolded one of the strangest mysteries ever to be brought to Holmes. The tale began in the seventeenth century with "a most wild, profane, and godless man" named Hugo Baskerville whose sins were to be punished by a "hound of hell . . . a great black beast, shaped like a hound, yet larger than any hound that ever mortal eye has rested upon." The spectre of the hound haunted the family for generations, and many Baskerville men were overtaken by sudden and violent death. The latest victim was Mortimer's friend, Sir Charles Baskerville, who had died of heart failure. In spite of an apparent natural cause of death, the country practitioner had observed nearby "the footprints of a gigantic hound."

Was the fearsome canine natural or supernatural? Would the new tenant of Baskerville Hall, the young Sir Henry, be threatened by the spectre? Could Holmes help?

Before the month was out, Holmes and Watson were to find themselves in an adventure so singular that Holmes's powers were pressed to their very limits. The *outré* chain of events led Holmes and Watson from Baker Street to Baskerville Hall, Dartmoor, and the unforgettable Grimpen Mire, all in pursuit of a villain so sinister that the Great Detective very nearly sacrificed young Baskerville's life before saving it.

The tale must have begun with a breakfast well suited to The Chase:

> Blackberries and Cream
> Eggs Baked with Chicken Livers
> Brioche
> Coffee

☞ Eggs Baked (Shirred) with Chicken Livers

Serves 6

6 whole chicken livers
Milk or buttermilk
2 tablespoons butter
12 tablespoons heavy cream
12 eggs
Several pinches of salt, pepper, paprika

Soak the chicken livers for 24 hours in milk or buttermilk. Cut the livers into pieces and fry them lightly in the butter. Distribute them in 12 buttered ramekins or custard cups. Add 1 tablespoon of heavy cream and 1 egg to each. Season with salt, pepper, and paprika. Place the ramekins in a water bath. Bake in a moderate oven (350°) for 10 to 15 minutes, or until the eggs are set but not hard.

Note: Instead of a tablespoon of cream, a pinch of dried dill and 1 tablespoon of cider may be added to each ramekin.

☞ **Brioche**

*Makes 1 loaf or
1 dozen brioche rolls*

    1 package dry yeast
    3 tablespoons warm water (105°–115°F.)
    3 teaspoons sugar
    1¾ cups flour
    3 freshly beaten large eggs
    1¼ teaspoons salt
    6 ounces softened butter
    1 beaten egg and 1 teaspoon water for egg wash

1) Dissolve the yeast and 1 teaspoon of sugar in the 3 tablespoons of warm water.

2) Place the flour in a bowl. Pour in the eggs. Add the rest of the sugar and salt and the yeast mixture.

3) Turn the mixture out on a lightly floured table. Knead it lightly, jus⁺ until the ingredients are completely mixed. Rest the dough for a few minutes. After the dough has rested, knead it until it becomes somewhat elastic. If the dough becomes too sticky, you may add up to 3 tablespoons of flour.

4) Begin kneading in the butter in small parcels. Continue kneading until the dough resumes its shape after being tapped. If the dough becomes too slippery, refrigerate it for a few minutes to solidify the butter. Allow the dough to rise to triple its original size.

5) Turn the dough out on a lightly floured surface. Punch it down; knead it again. Return it to a clean bowl. Allow it to rise again, this time to double its original volume.

6) Punch down the risen dough, and divide it among the brioche moulds. (Muffin tins may be used). To make the classic brioche shape, reserve ⅓ of the dough. Form the rest of the dough into balls, using about 2 tablespoons of dough for each one. Place each ball in a mould or muffin cup. Make a depression in the top of each ball. Mould the reserved dough

into balls, using about 1 tablespoon apiece. Place each of the small balls in the depression of one of the larger balls.

7) Allow them to rise to double their original size; brush the top of each with egg wash, and bake them in a 475°F. oven for about 15 minutes or until they are golden brown.

Note: It is necessary to allow at least 6 hours for the dough to rise and rest at the various stages along the way. This is in addition to the time you will spend actually handling and baking it. You may wish to let it stand, rising, in the refrigerator overnight.

The Sherlock Holmes Swiss Breakfast

No one can ever forget the stirring flight to Meiringen that culminated in the death struggle at Reichenbach Falls in "The Final Problem." Before the startling climax of this adventure, Holmes and Watson had spent several days enjoying the beauty of Switzerland.

On the third of May, 1891, they reached Meiringen, where they stayed at the Englischer Hof. The proprietor, Peter Steiler the elder, suggested that they would enjoy the hike over the hills to the hamlet of Rosenlaui, where they could spend the night. Furthermore, they were advised "on no account to pass the falls of Reichenbach, which are about halfway up the hills, without making a small detour to see them."

This they did, and Dr. Watson described the menacing waterfall: "It is, indeed, a fearful place. The torrent, swollen by the melting snow, plunges into a tremendous abyss, from which the spray rolls up like the smoke from a burning house. The shaft into which the river hurls itself is an immense chasm, lined by glistening coal-black rock, and narrowing into a creaming, boiling pit of incalculable depth, which brims over and shoots the stream onward over its jagged lip. The long sweep of green water roaring forever down, and the thick, flickering curtain of spray hissing forever upward, turn a man giddy with their constant whirl and clamour."

The rest is history; Watson was decoyed away from the spot. Sherlock Holmes met his arch foe, Professor Moriarty. The two locked in mortal combat, and the professor met his end at the bottom of the abyss. The civilized world breathed a sigh of relief at the demise of this Napoleon of crime, but any satisfaction was chilled by the report that Holmes had undone the wicked professor only at the cost of his own life. Alas, Watson said that Holmes and Moriarty went over the falls together. Only years later did a mournful public learn that Holmes did not, after all, perish at Reichenbach, but spent three years journeying to the far reaches of this planet, to return in 1894 to do battle with the remnants of the Moriarty gang.

We here re-create the breakfast of May 4, 1891, at Meiringen, before that fateful afternoon's journey. It was for three years to be remembered by Dr. Watson as the last he had shared with the man whom he described as "the best and the wisest man whom I have ever known."

This is a menu created for breakfast gourmets (which means late risers).

> Buttermilk
> Layered Egg Pancakes
> Fruit Compote
> Bircher Muesli
> Hot Chocolate

☞ Layered Egg Pancakes

Serves 4

3 cups all-purpose flour
½ teaspoon salt
3 eggs, well beaten
1¾ cups milk
4 hard-cooked eggs, shelled and left whole
Fat for deep frying

1) Sift the flour and salt together.

2) Beat in the eggs and milk until the batter is smooth and thick. Let it stand for 15 to 20 minutes.

3) Dip the hard-cooked eggs into the batter and fry them in deep hot

fat[1] (380°F.) for 2 to 3 minutes, or until they are golden brown. Drain them.

4) Dip the eggs again into the batter and fry them again to a golden brown.

5) Repeat the layering and frying until the batter is used up. There should be 4 to 5 layers on each egg.

6) Cut the eggs into pieces and serve them with a fruit compote.

Note: Cored but unpeeled whole apples may be used instead of eggs.

☞ Fruit Compote

Serves 4

12 ounces dried fruit (equal parts of apricots, peaches and apples)
2 cups water
1 stick cinnamon
Grated peel of 1 lemon
¼ cup sugar

1) Soak the dried fruit overnight in the 2 cups of water.

2) After the fruit has soaked, add the cinnamon, lemon peel and sugar.

3) Simmer it until the fruit is soft (approximately 25 to 30 minutes) and allow it to cool before serving.

☞ Bircher Muesli

Serves 4

¾ cup uncooked oatmeal
¾ cup cold water
¼ cup lemon juice
¼ cup honey or sweetened condensed milk
4 large unpeeled apples
½ cup chopped nuts

---

[1] On Sunday, October 25, 1891, the very year of the Great Encounter, the village of Meiringen was destroyed by fire. According to Philip S. Hench ("Of Violence at Meringen" in E. W. McDiarmid and Theodore C. Blegen's *Exploring Sherlock Holmes,* LaCrosse: Sumac Press, 1957), the blaze was set off by a mishap with deep hot fat during someone's Sunday breakfast preparations.

1) Soak the oatmeal in the cold water until it is soft (preferably over-night). It may be necessary to add more water later to make it the con-sistency of porridge. Instant oatmeal may be used, in which case it should be soaked for 10 minutes.

2) At serving time, stir in the lemon juice. Add the milk or honey.

3) Grate the apples coarsely directly into the mixture, and sprinkle nuts over it. Other fruits may be added if desired.

☞ **Hot Chocolate**

Serves 4

1 quart of milk
2 one-ounce squares of bitter chocolate
4 tablespoons sugar
A few grinds of salt
A few grains of cinnamon
Sweetened whipped cream (optional)

1) Pour the milk into the top of a double boiler. Grate or scrape the chocolate into it.

2) Heat it over hot water until the chocolate melts.

3) Add the sugar, salt, and cinnamon and beat thoroughly. Top each serving with slightly sweetened whipped cream, if desired.

The Wedding Breakfast

No treatise on Canonical breakfasts is complete without mention of the wedding breakfast of Lord Robert St. Simon. This is true, even though the meal was not strictly a breakfast; it was not served at Baker Street; nor was it eaten by Holmes and Watson. Nevertheless, it has a well-deserved place among the Canonical breakfasts, because it was at this meal that the mystery known as "The Adventure of the Noble Bachelor" began.

The wedding breakfast was given at the home of Mr. Aloysius Doran on the occasion of the marriage of his daughter, Hatty, to Lord Robert St. Simon, the second son of the Duke of Balmoral. The festive meal turned into a mystery when, after the guests had been seated, the bride suddenly vanished.

Tradition assigns this meal, a sort of brunch, the name "breakfast" because of the presumption that the members of the wedding party have neither time for, nor interest in, food before the nuptial vows are exchanged. At the wedding of Lord Robert St. Simon, there was little occasion to eat after the vows, either, owing to the bride's disappearance. Sherlock Holmes was commissioned to find her. He eventually solved the mystery to the satisfaction of everyone but the prospective bridegroom.

We regret that the guests were not able to fully enjoy the feast that marked the beginning of the mystery.

> Mushrooms with Tartar Sauce
> Jellied Eel
> Hashed Brown Potatoes
> Cold Veal and Ham Pie
> Piccalilly
> Stilton Cheese with Sherry Wine
> Maids of Honour
> Wedding Cake

☞ Mushrooms with Tartar Sauce

Serves 12

6 hard-cooked eggs
1 teaspoon salt, if necessary
8 grinds of pepper
¾ cup oil
Juice of ½ lemon
3 small pickles
3 tablespoons capers
4 tablespoons chopped chives
4 tablespoons chopped parsley
2 pounds medium-sized fresh mushrooms
4 eggs
¼ cup flour

1 cup breadcrumbs

3 cups vegetable shortening

1) Make the tartar sauce first: Press the hard-cooked egg yolks through a fine sieve, and season them with salt and pepper.

2) Slowly whip the oil into the egg yolks, drop by drop, until the mixture is smooth, like mayonnaise. Add a little lemon juice.

3) Chop the pickles and hard-cooked egg whites finely. Cut the capers in half and add them, together with the chopped chives and parsley, to the egg mixture.

4) Set the tartar sauce in the refrigerator to keep cool.

5) Wash and trim the mushrooms; dry them with a towel and cut them in half.

6) Whip the raw eggs and season them to taste with salt and pepper.

7) Dip the mushrooms into the flour, then into the whipped eggs, and then into the breadcrumbs.

8) Heat the vegetable shortening in a large pan. Add the mushrooms and fry them over medium heat for 5 minutes or until they are golden brown.

9) Serve the tartar sauce separately.

☞ Jellied Eel

Serves 12

3 pounds eel[1]

6 cups water, salted

1 large parsnip

1 large onion

1 herb bunch (5 stalks dill; 5 parsley stalks; 2 tarragon stalks, if
   available; 2 stalks of chervil or carrot greens)

2 bay leaves

1 teaspoon pickling spice

4 tablespoons vinegar

4 to 5 packages unflavoured gelatine

4 egg whites

2 carrots

---

[1] Recall the "high converse on eels and dace" in "The Adventure of Shoscombe Old Place." This recipe calls for fresh eel. Smoked eel (2 pounds) may be used to advantage, in which case the eel does not need to be cooked, and 6 cups of fish or chicken stock should be used to make the gelatine.

1) Peel and dice the parsnip and onion. Bring them to a boil in the salted water, along with the herb bunch, bay leaves, and pickling spice.

2) Add the eel and simmer it for 15 to 20 minutes.

3) Remove the eel from the broth and set it aside to cool.

4) Add the 4 tablespoons of vinegar and the gelatine to the 6 cups of broth to make aspic.[2] Season it well.

5) Clarify the liquid with the 4 egg whites. To do this, whip the egg whites to a meringue and whip them into the cold liquid aspic. Bring the aspic to a boil. Remove it from the heat and let it set for 6 minutes.

6) Strain carefully and cool.

7) Pour about a ½-inch layer of aspic into a round or rectangular mould and let it harden in the refrigerator.

8) Filet the eel and cut it into ½- to 1-inch pieces. Boil the carrots and slice them.

9) Set the eel pieces on the jellied aspic, and decorate with carrot slices. Pour the rest of the aspic over the eel pieces. Cool, unmould and serve.

☞ Hashed Brown Potatoes

Serves 12

1 dozen large potatoes
1½ onions
Fat for frying

1) Cook the potatoes, leaving them slightly underdone. In order to produce a truly superior result, cook the potatoes the day before and have them as dry and mealy as possible.

2) Grate the potatoes and chop the onions.

3) Pan-fry the potatoes with the onions until they are crisp.

☞ Cold Veal and Ham Pie

Serves 12

2 tablespoons softened butter
2 pounds lean boneless veal, cut into ¼-inch cubes
1 pound lean smoked ham, cut into ¼-inch cubes

[2] Test the mixture by putting a small spoonful in a dish in the refrigerator. If it does not jell, add more gelatine.

¼ cup chopped parsley
5 to 6 tablespoons brandy
5 to 6 tablespoons chicken or beef stock (may be fresh or canned)
1 to 2 tablespoons lemon juice
1 teaspoon lemon peel
½ to 1 teaspoon crumbled dried sage leaves
½ teaspoon salt, or to taste
¼ teaspoon ground black pepper
Hot Water Crust (see recipe, page 48)
4 hard-boiled eggs
1 egg yolk combined with 1 tablespoon heavy cream for egg wash
2 cups fresh or canned chicken stock, chilled
3 envelopes unflavoured gelatine

1) Preheat the oven to 350°F. Using a pastry brush, coat the bottom and sides of a 10 by 5 by 4-inch loaf pan with butter. Set the pan aside.

2) Combine the veal, ham, parsley, brandy, stock, lemon juice, lemon peel, sage, salt, and pepper in a large bowl. Toss the ingredients about with a spoon until they are thoroughly mixed.

3) Prepare the Hot Water Crust according to the recipe below. Break off about ⅓ of the pastry and set it aside. Roll out the remaining dough on a lightly floured surface. Roll it into a rectangle about 20 inches long, 10 inches wide and ⅓ inch thick.

4) Drape the pastry over a rolling pin and lift it up. Unroll it slackly over the loaf pan. Press the pastry into the pan, gently, with a dull object. Then roll the pin over the rim to trim off the excess pastry.

5) Fill the pan a little less than half full with the veal-and-ham mixture. Arrange the peeled whole hard-boiled eggs in a single row down the center of the pan. Cover the eggs with the remaining meat mixture, filling the pastry shell to within 1 inch of the top.

6) Roll the reserved pastry dough into a 4 by 15-inch rectangle. Lift it up on the pin and drape it over the top of the mixture. Trim off the excess with a paring knife. Crimp the pastry securely to the rim of the pan with a fork or with your fingers.

7) Cut a 1-inch round hole in the center of the pie. Roll out any scraps of dough and cut into oval leaf and flower shapes. Moisten the bottoms and sides with egg wash and arrange them on the pie. Brush the entire pie with egg wash. Cover the top of the pie with a lid or a piece of aluminum foil laid loosely over the top.

8) Bake the pie in the middle of a 350°F. oven for 2 hours, or until the top is golden brown. Remove it from the oven and cool it for 20 minutes.

9) Mix the 2 cups of cold chicken stock and the gelatine powder in a saucepan. Allow the powder to dissolve for 3 to 4 minutes over low heat. Season the mixture to taste and allow it to cool.

10) Pour the gelatine (aspic) through a funnel into the opening of the pie. Cool the pie at room temperature, then refrigerate it overnight or until the aspic has set.

11) To unmould the pie, run the blade of a sharp knife around the inside edge of the pan, and dip the bottom of the pan in hot water. Wipe the pan dry, place a serving dish over it, and, grasping the pan and plate together firmly, turn them over quickly. Tap the plate on a table, and the pie should slide out easily. Turn the pie over, and cut it into 1/2-inch-thick slices. Serve it with mustard vegetables (piccalilly).

HOT WATER CRUST

*Makes approximately
1 pound*

    2 cups flour
    1/4 teaspoon coarse (Kosher) salt
    1 cup milk or water, or milk and water
    1/4 cup pork lard or vegetable shortening

1) Mix the flour and salt in a bowl.

2) Heat the milk and the shortening together until the shortening is melted. Pour it slowly over the flour.

3) Mix it with a wooden spoon until it is of a uniform doughy consistency.

4) Work the dough for 3 to 4 minutes until it is smooth and does not stick to the board.

5) Roll the dough out and press it into a pie dish.

☞ Piccalilly

Fills eight 1-pint jars

    1 small head cauliflower
    3 medium-sized green tomatoes (1 pound)
    2 medium-sized zucchini squash, halved (1 pound)
    2 medium-sized cucumbers
    1 to 2 tablespoons coarse salt
    4 cups vinegar

½ cup dry mustard
¼ cup curry powder or turmeric
2 tablespoons flour
½ cup sugar

1) Separate the cauliflower into florets, and cut the tomatoes, squash, and cucumbers into thin slices.

2) Put the vegetables and salt into a large bowl in layers. Cover the bowl with a towel and allow it to rest overnight.

3) The next day, rinse and drain the vegetables. Toss them in a cloth to dry them.

4) Blend 1 cup of vinegar with the mustard, turmeric and flour, until it is a smooth paste.

5) Combine the rest of the vinegar with the sugar in a large kettle.

6) Heat it to a boil, and boil it for 5 to 6 minutes.

7) Add the vegetables and cook them for 10 minutes. Stir in the mustard paste and simmer for 5 minutes longer.

8) Spoon the piccalilly into sterilized jars and seal them.

9) Put the jars in a boiling-water bath: place them on a trivet in a large kettle of water that reaches one-half to three-fourths of the way up the sides of the jars and boil for 20 minutes.

☞ Maids of Honour

Makes 12

¾ cup sweet butter
1½ cups all-purpose flour
2½ teaspoons salt
1 hard-cooked egg yolk, grated
5 raw egg yolks
⅔ cup sugar
2 teaspoons grated lemon rind
¼ pound pot or farmer cheese
3 tablespoons ground blanched almonds
Juice of ½ lemon
¼ teaspoon nutmeg

1) Soften ½ cup of the butter.

2) Put the flour in a large bowl or on a board. Make a well in the centre of the flour. In the well, add the ½ cup of softened butter, 1 teaspoon of salt, the grated hard-cooked egg yolk, 1 raw egg yolk, 2 tablespoons of sugar, and 1 teaspoon of grated lemon rind.

3) Work these ingredients into the flour with your fingers, starting at the centre and working outward in a spiral motion, and kneading them together until all the flour has been absorbed.

4) Roll the dough into a ball and chill it in the refrigerator.

5) Cream the remaining butter until it is light, and beat in the pot cheese. Beat in all the remaining ingredients except the nutmeg.

6) Remove the chilled dough from the refrigerator and divide it into 12 equal pieces.

7) Press each piece against the bottom and sides of a 3-inch-diameter tart or muffin pan. (The dough will be too crumbly to roll out effectively.)

8) Fill each shell approximately ⅔ full with the cheese mixture, and sprinkle each with a little nutmeg.

9) Bake them in a 350°F. oven until the tarts are brown and the filling is just set, about 25 minutes. Remove them from the oven, and unmould them while they are still warm.

☞ Wedding Cake

Makes one 4-pound or two 2-pound fruitcakes

⅓ cup light clover honey
4 ounces dry sherry (½ cup)
2 cups light raisins
2 cups dark raisins
3 cups chopped candied mixed fruit
⅓ cup chopped candied cherries
½ cup plus 1 tablespoon granulated sugar
¾ cup vegetable shortening
3 medium-sized eggs
1⅓ cups all-purpose flour
⅛ teaspoon cinnamon
⅛ teaspoon ground cloves
⅛ teaspoon ginger
⅛ teaspoon salt
⅔ cup chopped walnuts

1) Mix the honey and sherry together. Add the fruit, tossing it until it is completely coated. Cover it and marinate it at room temperature for at least 24 hours. Stir it occasionally.

2) Mix the sugar and shortening with an electric mixer at medium

speed for 2 minutes. Do not overbeat it. Add the eggs slowly, and blend them in.

3) Sift the dry ingredients together, and add them to the batter. Mix them at medium speed with an electric mixer for 4 minutes. Do not overbeat.

4) Fold in the marinated fruit, the marinade, and the walnuts. Mix well to coat all the fruit with the batter.

5) Line the cake pan (s) with waxed paper. Fill completely, for the cake will not rise.

6) Bake the cake in a preheated 300°F. oven. If baked in two 7 by 2½ by 3-inch pans, it should be baked for 40 to 60 minutes. If baked in a single circular 7-inch-diameter by 3-inch pan, it should be baked for 80 to 90 minutes. In any event, the cake should be firm in the centre before it is removed from the oven. It is advisable to place a piece of foil over it during the last stages of baking.

BUTTER CREAM ICING

Traditionally, the wedding cake combined a sweet royal icing with a bitter-almond marzipan, symbolic of the bittersweet nature of marriage. The following is a modern-day substitute, an easy almond icing.

>3 tablespoons butter
>1½ cups confectioners' sugar
>3 or more teaspoons light cream
>½ teaspoon almond flavouring
>Pinch of salt

Beat the butter at room temperature until it is creamy. Sift the sugar and add it to the butter slowly, together with the cream. Add the almond flavouring and the salt and beat until fluffy.

☞

"A Singular Set of Recipes, Watson"

The Sherlock Holmes tales abound in references to mealtimes, but offer few references to specific items of food. The Complete Holmesian Culinary Picture nevertheless brings to mind certain specific dishes which merit individual attention. It is a singular collection. Each of the items has its own *raison d'être*, whether it be a food mentioned in the stories, a reminder of a particular Canonical character, or an outgrowth of a phrase which begs gustatory amplification. As in the case of all the recipes in the book, they are served up with a dash of logic, a pinch of chronology, and a few grinds of research. We hope the reader finds the result agreeable.

Oysters Athelney Jones[1]

"Shall the world, then, be overrun by oysters?" asked Sherlock Holmes in mock delirium during "The Adventure of the Dying Detective." Perhaps not the world, but the cuisine of Victorian England was fairly overrun by this delicious mollusk—but only in season. By law the availability of oysters was restricted to the period of September through April, or, by convenient mnemonic, the months with an "r" in them. Holmes could

[1] This was one of the delicacies on the dinner menu commemorating Sherlock Holmes at the Culinary Institute of America, June 2, 1973.

allow the proliferation of oysters, but not the spread of villainy, which unfortunately knew no season. Better the world be overrun by oysters than by the Moriartys, Morans, Milvertons, Culverton Smiths, and others of their kidney. Doubtless, Detective Athelney Jones, who shared oysters with Holmes and Watson during *The Sign of Four,* would have agreed.

☞ **Oysters Athelney Jones**

Serves 10

30 oysters
9 medium-sized mushrooms
Lemon juice
Melted butter
Breadcrumbs

1) Open the oysters. Gently pry them away from the shell without tearing the flesh.

2) Poach the oysters by putting them in a pan with their own liquid which has been strained through a cheesecloth.

3) Bring them to a boil. As soon as the liquid begins to bubble, remove the pan from the stove and allow it to cool.

4) Cut the mushrooms into 4 slices each, and alternate the oysters and mushrooms on a skewer. Season them with lemon juice, and dip them in melted butter. Sprinkle them with breadcrumbs and brown them lightly under the broiler. Serve with toothpicks.

Prawn Salad Ryder[1]

If the Holmesian world were to be overrun by oysters, as the Master exclaimed in "The Adventure of the Dying Detective," then prawns would be right with them to share their pre-eminence. Prawns, or shrimp,

[1] This was one of the items on the menu at the Sherlock Holmes commemorative dinner of June 2, 1973, at the Culinary Institute of America.

appeared in mid-nineteenth-century cuisine in legions as numerous as oysters,[2] and they were the most plentiful when oysters could not be had. There is no direct evidence in any of the Holmes stories that Holmes ever ate prawns. Their place among Sherlockian cuisine is won by Holmes's having referred to the rascal Ryder as a shrimp, in "The Adventure of the Blue Carbuncle."

☞ Prawn Salad Ryder

Serves 4

  1 pound of prawns or shrimp, cooked and peeled
  6 tablespoons oil
  2 tablespoons vinegar
  Salt, pepper, or paprika
  1 to 2 cloves garlic
  12 mushrooms, sliced
  3 tomatoes, sliced
  1 small can of asparagus, drained (10½ ounces)
  2 hard-boiled eggs, cut in wedges
  1 head of lettuce, shredded

1) Combine the oil, vinegar, and seasonings by shaking them or by whisking them together. Crush the garlic with salt and add to the mixture.

2) Put the prawns and mushrooms in a bowl. Coat them with the dressing, and leave them in a cool place for 50 to 60 minutes. Garnish them with tomatoes, asparagus, eggs, and lettuce.

The Trout in the Milk

"Circumstantial evidence is occasionally very convincing, as when you find a trout in the milk," said Sherlock Holmes, "to quote Thoreau's ex-

---

[2] Should there be any doubt as to this fact, reference to H. Mayhew, *London Labour and the London Poor*, 1851, *1*, p. 63, will show that 489,428,468 shrimp were sold in Billingsgate Market in the year 1851, as opposed to 495,896,000 oysters!

ample."[1] With this statement the Master revealed his knowledge of a common food-adulteration practice of his day, that of scooping water out of a stream in order to dilute the milk. Modern chemical means of estimating the amount of butterfat in milk have counteracted this old scheme.

The food adulteration of Holmes's time was at least as poisonous as that of our own: alum in bread, copperas (ferrous sulphate) in beer, lead and copper salts in confectionery for children. The list is long and outrageous. Those of us who long for a simpler, more "organic" cuisine than is available today do not long for the gas-lit tranquillity of the Victorian dining table.

In honour of Holmes's awareness of culinary rascality, we propose a dish to be named "The Trout in the Milk," or "Trout à la Thoreau." Trout which is simply poached in milk will not suffice, for the fish and milk, by themselves, do little to enhance each other. When the milk is incorporated into a cream sauce, however, that is another matter.

☞ The Trout in the Milk

Serves 4

4 trout (6 to 8 ounces each), fresh if possible
2 shallots, chopped
1 ⅓ teaspoons salt, or to taste
Juice of ½ lemon
⅓ cup water
⅓ cup milk
2 cups heavy cream
8 slices tomato
2 teaspoons chopped hazelnuts
Butter

1) Butter a baking dish and sprinkle it with the chopped shallots. Place the cleaned trout on top. Season with a little salt, sprinkle with a little lemon juice, and add the ⅓ cup of water and ⅓ cup of milk.

2) Cover the fish with a buttered paper, and poach it in the oven at 400°F for 5 to 8 minutes.

3) Pour off the stock into a saucepan (keep trout warm). Add the cream to the stock, and simmer it until it is reduced in volume by one-half to one-third.

4) Sauté the tomato slices for 30 seconds on each side in butter, and

1 "The Adventure of the Noble Bachelor."

place them on top of the trout. Pour the sauce over the top, and sprinkle with the chopped hazelnuts. Serve with blanched broccoli and boiled fine noodles.

Galantine of Pork with Sauce Oxford or Sauce Cambridge[1]

In the beginning of July 1895, a passerby to Allardyce's back shop might have witnessed a remarkable sight: Sherlock Holmes in his shirtsleeves grasping a harpoon, furiously stabbing at a dead pig which swung from a hook in the ceiling. He learned, by the most direct means possible, that no matter how hard he tried, he could not "transfix the pig with a single blow." All this had a definite bearing upon his judgement of the means by which sea-captain Peter Carey had met his most gruesome death. Not all pigs in Holmes's era were made to suffer the indignities of Holmes's experimental one. Most found their way to Victorian dining tables; some, we fancy, reappearing as Galantine of Pork. Because we do not intend to rekindle the controversy pertaining to the college that Holmes attended, we offer a choice of two sauces as an accompaniment: Sauce Oxford and Sauce Cambridge.

☞ **Galantine of Pork**

Serves 10 to 12

> 2 pounds breast of pork
> 1/2 to 1 teaspoon salt
> 2 to 3 pinches white pepper

---

[1] Galantine of Pork with Sauce Oxford was served at the Culinary Institute dinner of June 2, 1973. Sauce Cambridge has been added in this volume for the sake of neutrality. At any one meal, either one sauce or the other should be served, not both.

Stuffing:

> 6 ounces lean pork or veal, chilled
> 1 egg white
> ⅓ teaspoon salt, or to taste
> A pinch of pepper
> 7 to 10 tablespoons heavy cream
> 2 ounces smoked ham or smoked beef tongue, diced
> 1 tablespoon flour
> 1 tablespoon pistachio nuts (optional)
> 1 truffle (optional)

1) Have the butcher trim the meat and remove the rib bones.

2) Prepare a stuffing by grinding the chilled lean pork or veal thoroughly and combining it in a blender or food chopper with the egg white, seasonings, and heavy cream. Keep it cold the whole time.

3) Fold into the stuffing the smoked ham, the flour, and any of the optional ingredients.

4) If the breast is thin, spread the stuffing over the inside of the meat; then roll it and tie it up. If the breast is thick, have the butcher make an incision (pouch) in it. Put the filling in this and sew it together.

5) Season the meat with the salt and white pepper, and place it on a rack in a roasting pan. Roast it in the oven, without basting it or adding any liquid, at 350°F. for 1½ to 2 hours, or until done. On a meat thermometer, the internal temperature should be 170°F.

6) Cool it overnight, remove threads and strings, and slice it thinly.

SAUCE OXFORD

*Makes approximately
½ cup*

> 2 tablespoons red currant jelly
> 2 tablespoons port, sherry, or Madeira wine
> 3 tablespoons red wine
> Juice of 1 lemon or orange
> ½ teaspoon dry mustard
> A pinch of cayenne pepper
> A pinch of ginger
> 1 tablespoon grated orange or lemon peel

Stir the jelly over gentle heat until it dissolves. Add the wine, fruit juice, and spices. Bring it to a boil, and simmer it for 5 to 10 minutes. Add the grated peel, and bring to a boil again. Serve it cold.

SAUCE CAMBRIDGE

Makes approximately
½ cup

2 hard-cooked egg yolks
½ teaspoon mustard
1 mashed anchovy fillet
1 teaspoon vinegar
⅓ teaspoon salt, or to taste
¾ cup oil
1 tablespoon of a mixture of finely chopped capers and gherkins
1 teaspoon of a mixture of chopped fresh chervil, tarragon, and
   parsley

1) Pass the egg yolks through a sieve.
2) Mix the egg yolk with the mustard, anchovy, and vinegar. Season it
with salt and combine it with the oil, one drop at a time, until it is all
thoroughly mixed.
3) Stir in the remaining ingredients. Taste and adjust the seasoning.

Veal Cutlet Coram

Who killed young Willoughby Smith, the secretary to elderly Professor
Coram? There was no apparent motive for the foul murder. There were
only a couple of clues: a pair of very strong eyeglasses which gave this case
the name, "The Adventure of the Golden Pince-Nez," and the dying
words of the murdered man, "The professor, it was she." That was all
that Inspector Stanley Hopkins had to go on when he asked Holmes and
Watson to investigate Yoxley Old Place with him. Holmes, of course,
discovered many more clues, not the least of which was the hearty
luncheon of cutlets ordered by the ailing, chain-smoking professor. After
he had deduced the inescapable solution to the mystery, Holmes waited
until he and Dr. Watson had eaten some cutlets, too, before he dra-
matically unveiled the murderer.

☞ Veal Cutlet Coram

Serves 4

4 veal cutlets, 7 to 8 ounces each
Salt and black pepper to taste
2 tablespoons flour
3½ ounces butter
⅛ cup white wine
1½ bunches parsley
3 stems chervil
3 stems tarragon
½ cup hot beef broth
2 tomatoes

1) Rinse the veal cutlets and dry them with a towel. Flatten them lightly, season with salt and pepper, and turn them in flour, pressing the cutlets into the flour.

2) Heat half of the butter in a pan and sauté the cutlets for 5 minutes on each side, or until they are golden brown.

3) Set the cutlets on a warm tray, keeping them warm. Deglaze the pan with white wine, and bring to a boil.

4) Wash 1 bunch of parsley, the chervil, and the tarragon, and dry the herbs with a towel. Chop them finely. Add them to the boiling liquid. Add the meat stock and boil for 15 minutes.

5) Whip the rest of the butter into the sauce and pour it over the cutlets. Garnish the cutlets with the rest of the parsley and with the tomatoes, cut into wedges.

Chicken Breasts Murillo

In the world of cuisine, a gourmet dish was once created to honor the Spanish painter Bartolomé Esteban Murillo (1617–1682). The name Murillo has Holmesian connotations as well, for it was Don Juan Murillo, alias "The Tiger of San Pedro," whose villainy marked "The Adventure of Wisteria Lodge."

The tyrant Murillo fled England as Holmes and Baynes of the Surrey Constabulary, each working independently, closed in on him, at the culmination of an adventure which had produced a plethora of grotesque clues, among them a mutilated white cock. Appropriately enough, the dish named for Murillo[1] is also a gallinaceous fowl. Whether it be coincidence or consanguinity, the connection is inescapable. It points unerringly toward the inclusion of a suitable chicken dish in (dis)honour of Don Juan Murillo, the Tiger of San Pedro.

☞ Chicken Breasts Murillo

Serves 4

4 boneless chicken breasts
½ teaspoon salt
⅓ to ½ teaspoon pepper
4 to 5 ounces butter
12 mushroom caps
2 shallots, chopped fine
⅓ bottle white wine
½ cup heavy cream
½ pound fine noodles

1) Cut each chicken breast into 4 pieces.

2) Season the chicken pieces, and brown them on both sides in 2 ounces of hot butter.

3) Add the mushrooms; cook them with the chicken, covered, in a 350° to 375°F. oven until the chicken is done.

4) Arrange the chicken pieces and mushrooms in a dish and keep them hot.

5) Fry the shallots lightly in 1 ounce of butter. Add the white wine and boil it down to half the volume. Add the cream and cook until the sauce is creamy. Pour it over the chicken.

6) Cook the fine noodles according to package directions. Toss them in 1 to 2 ounces of butter, and garnish the chicken with them.

[1] Described by Dietman Barnikell in "A Biographical Sketch of Who Is Who on the Menu," published serially in *The Culinarian*, the official publication of the Chefs' Association of the Pacific Coast.

Something Nutritious at Simpson's

Several restaurants are mentioned in the Canon, but Simpson's-in-the-Strand was a special favourite of the Great Detective's. Holmes and Watson dined there so often that in "The Adventure of the Illustrious Client" Watson referred to it as *"our* Strand restaurant" (emphasis ours), and during that adventure, they dined there not once but twice. It was to Simpson's that Holmes repaired with Watson during "The Adventure of the Dying Detective" for "something nutritious" after he had fasted for several days. By a masterful feat of malingering, Holmes had just lured the murderous Culverton Smith into confessing his heinous crimes.

When Simpson's-in-the-Strand first opened, it was a "home of chess." Some years later, before adopting the name by which it was known to Holmes and Watson, it was referred to as the "Grand Cigar Divan." The cigars suited Holmes and Watson well, for both were inveterate smokers. There is no evidence, however, that they ever went to Simpson's because of the chess. Indeed, in "The Adventure of the Retired Colourman," Holmes expressed his clear scorn of the game and its enthusiasts: ". . . one mark, Watson, of a scheming mind."

There is a curious problem concerning Holmes's and Watson's dining at Simpson's-in-the-Strand during "The Adventure of the Illustrious Client." Watson had stated clearly that the adventure began on September 3, 1902. Simpson's was demolished in 1900 when the Strand was widened, and the rebuilding and remodeling were not complete until 1904. Did Watson deliberately fabricate the date? Had he forgotten where they actually had eaten? Alas, it will remain forever a mystery.

Simpson's is still in the Strand. The atmosphere within its walls has changed little since 1904. The restaurant's general manager, Mr. A. P. J. Mumford, graciously provided us with some historical details about the restaurant, and the Master Cook, Mr. Joseph Curley, has offered us the following traditional recipe to represent what Holmes and Watson might have eaten there:

KENTISH CAPON PUDDING

"Breast of Capon, and salt meat of young porker, scallions, chopped parsley, seasoning, stock from capon.

"Line pie basin with suet crust, place in the above ingredients, and cover with crust; tie with cloth and boil for 2½ hours.

"Serve with creamed chicken and parsley sauce."

We have taken the liberty of adding some details of our own and offering the following instructions for the estimable Victorian treat:

☞ Kentish Capon Pudding

Serves 4

2 cups flour
1 teaspoon baking powder
⅓ teaspoon salt
¼ pound ground suet
Cold water to mix (about ⅓ cup)
1½ pounds breast of capon
1 pound lean slab bacon, cubed
6 scallions, coarsely cut
8 grinds of black pepper

White Sauce:
3 tablespoons butter
3 tablespoons flour
3 to 4 cups chicken stock
1½ teaspoons salt, or to taste
2 tablespoons chopped fresh parsley

1) Sift the flour, baking powder and salt together into a bowl. Add the ground suet and mix together well. Add enough water to make a soft but not sticky dough.

2) Grease a fireproof mould, bowl, or casserole (about 1 to 1½ quarts), and line it with the dough, reserving ⅓ of the dough to cover the pudding.

3) Cube the capon breast and mix it with the cubed slab bacon, scallions, some salt, and the pepper.

4) Fill the crust with the mixture, moisten the edges of the crust with water, and cover it with the reserved dough.

5) Tie the whole thing tightly in a cheesecloth that has been greased on one side, and boil it for 2½ hours. (This pudding may be boiled in the same manner as the Christmas Plum Pudding, see p. 169.)

6) While the pudding is boiling, prepare a White Sauce: melt the 3 tablespoons of butter in a large saucepan. Add the 3 tablespoons of flour and stir together to make a roux. Add about 4 cups of chicken stock and cook until the sauce begins to thicken. Taste it, adjust the seasoning, and add the parsley. Serve it with the pudding, which should be served in the casserole in which it was cooked.

Steak Tonga

In *The Sign of Four,* Holmes and Watson encountered one of the most curious persons of their entire saga, the Andaman Islander named Tonga, companion to Englishman Jonathan Small. A diminutive aborigine with a huge misshapen head, a mass of tangled hair, and a quiver full of poison darts,[1] teamed with an embittered one-legged escaped convict were formidable adversaries to Holmes, Watson, and the band of street urchins known as the Baker Street Irregulars. Before coming to the attention of the Great Detective, Tonga and Small had wandered throughout England while the tiny islander earned their living as a carnival exhibit: "He would eat raw meat and dance his war dance." No mention is made of the type or cut of meat that Tonga consumed to the amusement of onlookers, but we commemorate him with raw meat prepared as follows:

☞ **Steak Tonga**

Serves 2

1 pound raw lean beef, ground
2 eggs

---

[1] Curiously, the Andaman Islanders did not use poison darts, and they were meticulous in grooming their short-cropped hair. For more about Tonga's dubious identity, see Julia Rosenblatt, "Who Was Tonga and Why Were They Saying Such Terrible Things About Him?" *Baker Street Journal,* 1975, 25, pp. 140–141.

1 teaspoon paprika
1 teaspoon salt
1/3 teaspoon pepper
2 tablespoons chopped onions
2 tablespoons chopped pickles
1 teaspoon prepared mustard
1/2 teaspoon white vinegar or 1 teaspoon rum or brandy

Mix well and serve on rye or pumpernickel bread.

The Cornish Horror

"Why not tell them of the Cornish horror—strangest case I have handled," suggested Holmes to Watson some years after the event. During a vacation in Cornwall, described in "The Adventure of the Devil's Foot," Holmes solved a bizarre mystery in an investigation which almost cost the lives of our beloved pair. The mystery, however, was but an interruption of Holmes's archaeological studies. In the words of Watson, "The glamour and mystery of the place, with its sinister atmosphere of forgotten nations, appealed to the imagination of my friend. . . . The ancient Cornish language had also arrested his attention, and he had, I remember, conceived the idea that it was akin to the Chaldean, and had been largely derived from the Phoenician traders in tin." We can only speculate whether, having noted some linguistic connection with Phoenicia, Holmes observed any gastronomic influence as well. He no doubt partook of a local specialty, the Cornish pasty, finding it particularly fitting for sustenance during his "long walks and solitary meditations upon the moor." Observed one culinary source, "In my youth every knowing man and boy put a meat pasty in his pocket when going for a day's tramp or hunt . . . but what of the form of the pasty? Why this; it was not unlike two Phrygian caps put together at their base. In other words it was like a quarter moon with somewhat blunted horns—in fact the emblem of Astarte, goddess of the Phoenicians."[1]

[1] Mr. John Pollock, quoted in Florence White, *Good Things in England*, London: Jonathan Cape, 1932.

☞ **Cornish Pasty**

Makes 3 pasties

2 cups flour
3 ounces lard or shortening (a little less than ½ cup)
A pinch of salt
⅓ to ½ cup water

Flake the flour and lard together. Add the salt and water. Work the mixture into a smooth dough and allow it to rest under a cover for 30 minutes.

Prepare the filling:

¼ pound beef liver or chicken liver
½ pound ground beef
Salt and pepper to taste
2 raw potatoes
1 small onion
1 small carrot
1 rib of celery
1 small turnip (optional)
1 egg, beaten

1) Chop the liver coarsely in a blender and mix it with the ground beef. Add salt and pepper. Allow it to rest for 10 to 20 minutes.

2) Peel the onion and pare the potato, carrot, and turnip. Slice them and the celery thinly and blanch them in boiling water for 2 to 3 minutes. Drain them and cool them in ice water. Drain them again and dry them on a cloth. Season them with salt and pepper.

3) Roll out the dough to ⅛- to ⅓-inch thickness.[2] Cut it into three large squares. Put a layer of vegetables on half of each square of dough and top it with some of the meat mixture.

4) Brush the edges of the dough with egg wash (1 beaten egg), and fold the plain half over the meat. Pinch the edges together *tightly*.

5) Bake the pasties for 1 hour. Start the baking at 400°F. for 2 to 3 minutes. Then quickly turn the oven down to 300° to 325°F. for the rest of the hour. Check the oven temperature carefully. If the temperature does not drop quickly, lower the setting to 250° and leave the oven door open until the desired temperature is reached.

[2] Authenticity would argue for the thinner dough. We suggest the thicker because it is easier to handle and therefore more likely to produce a successful result.

Medallion of Beef Montpensier

In many of his cases, Holmes brought justice to the land not so much by finding the criminal but by clearing the name of an innocent accused. Holmes was always undaunted: "There is nothing more stimulating than a case where everything goes against you."[1] A host of suspects had Holmes to thank that they were not among those unfortunate souls who were made to pay for crimes that others committed, or, for that matter, crimes that were never committed at all. For example, in a case that Watson never fully published, Holmes "defended the unfortunate Mme. Montpensier from the charge of murder which hung over her in connection with the death of her step-daughter, Mlle. Carère, the young lady who, as it will be remembered, was found six months later alive and married in New York."[2] In the world of classical cuisine, the garniture Montpensier was allegedly named in honour of Anne Marie Louise d'Orleans, Duchesse de Montpensier.[3] We present it here in honour of Sherlock Holmes, defender of the innocent.

☞ **Medallion of Beef Montpensier**

Serves 4

8 fillets of beef, center cut (4 ounces each)
3 tablespoons fresh butter or oil
8 green asparagus tips (canned, fresh, or frozen)
2 finely diced shallots
⅓ cup white wine
1 cup of Brown Sauce (see recipe, p. 159)
8 grinds of pepper

[1] *The Hound of the Baskervilles.*
[2] *Ibid.*
[3] Henry Smith, *Classical Recipes of the World,* New York: Macmillan, 1955.

1 teaspoon salt

8 truffle slices (optional)

1) Salt the fillets very slightly. Heat 2 tablespoons of the butter or oil, and sauté the fillets. Cook them medium to rare.

2) Meanwhile, if fresh or frozen asparagus is used, cook it. If canned, warm it in slightly seasoned water.

3) When the fillets are ready, remove them from the pan and keep them warm.

4) Add the shallots to the pan and sauté them for a second. Add the wine and reduce it in volume by one-half. Add the Brown Sauce and simmer it for 5 minutes.

5) Strain the sauce and fold in the remaining butter. Adjust the seasoning by adding the pepper and 1 teaspoon of salt, if needed.

6) Cover the fillets with the sauce. Top each with an asparagus tip, cut in half lengthwise, and with a truffle slice. Serve with rice or Duchess Potatoes (see recipe, p. 124).

Note: The fillets may be rolled in bacon before they are sautéed. Crawfish tail may be substituted for each truffle slice.

Ned Hunter's Curried Mutton

Curried mutton is a tasty dish indeed. So tasty, that in "Silver Blaze" it provided the ideal vehicle for the drug that rendered stable-boy Ned Hunter unconscious the night that the famed racehorse, Silver Blaze, disappeared. Explained Sherlock Holmes, "Powdered opium is by no means tasteless. The flavour is not disagreeable, but it is perceptible. Were it mixed with any ordinary dish, the eater would undoubtedly detect it and would probably eat no more. A curry was exactly the medium which would disguise the taste." Here follows a recipe for a delicious supper of curried mutton. We have omitted the opium. If the reader wishes to include it, we recommend a small dosage to be added after the curry is cooked. In that case, the subsequent courses of the meal may be omitted.

☞ **Curried Mutton**

Serves 4

1 pound lamb[1]
2 ounces butter
2 onions, finely chopped
1 bay leaf
3 cloves
Meat broth to cover meat, plus 5 cups
2 cups uncooked rice
10 almonds
3 teaspoons curry powder
1 to 1½ teaspoons salt, or to taste
Juice of 1 lemon

1) Cut the lamb into fine strips or small cubes.

2) Melt the butter and sauté the onions until they are transparent.

3) Add the meat, bay leaf, and cloves. Add enough meat broth just to cover meat, and simmer it for 20 minutes.

4) Remove the spices. Add the rice, almonds, and the 5 cups of meat broth. Boil for 10 minutes.

5) Season the dish with curry powder, salt, and lemon juice. Bring it to a boil, cover it, and remove it from the fire. Allow it to rest for 10 to 15 minutes, or until the rice has cooked.

Baskerville Beef Tongue, Sauce Chantilly[2]

In *The Hound of the Baskervilles,* Holmes the ascetic camped on Dartmoor in a neolithic stone hut, secretly investigating the terrifying

---

[1] Recognizing the American preference for lamb, we have made this substitution for mutton.

[2] This was one of the menu items for the Culinary Institute of America's Sherlock Holmes dinner on June 2, 1973. Four to six calves' tongues or pigs' tongues may be used instead of beef tongue, in which case reduce the cooking time to 1½ hours for calves' tongues and 2 hours for pigs' tongues.

spectre of the hound of hell. When Watson first encountered his friend's rude quarters, ". . . a litter of empty tins showed that the place had been occupied for some time. . . . In the middle of the hut a flat stone served the purpose of a table, and upon this stood a small cloth bundle. . . . It contained a loaf of bread, a tinned tongue, and two tins of preserved peaches." It was this rude provision that inspired this dish:

☞ Baskerville Beef Tongue

Serves 8 to 10

1 beef tongue (2 to 3 pounds)
Water
Salt (if fresh tongue is used)
6 white peppercorns
6 whole allspice
1 small bay leaf
1 carrot, sliced
1 onion, sliced

1) Put the tongue into a saucepan and cover it well with water. (If the tongue has been salted previously, it should be soaked for 24 hours in water, and no further salt added.)

2) Bring it to a boil, skim it, and add the seasonings, bay leaf, carrot, and onion. Cover the pan and simmer for 3 hours.

3) Pull the skin off the tongue while it is still hot. Cool the tongue in the stock. Slice it thinly from the root to the tip. Serve it cold with Sauce Chantilly. Sauce Chantilly is sometimes referred to as a mousseline sauce and as such may be taken to commemorate the *mousseline-de-soie* worn by Mrs. Neville St. Clair in "The Man with the Twisted Lip."

SAUCE CHANTILLY

Makes 1½ cups

1 cup mayonnaise
½ cup whipped cream
1½ tablespoons grated horseradish

Mix these ingredients together.

Mrs. Barrymore's Potato Cakes

While Sherlock Holmes stealthily camped on the moor, Dr. Watson joined Sir Henry Baskerville at Baskerville Hall, where the butler and house-keeper, Mr. and Mrs. Barrymore, did their utmost to make them comfortable. We have discovered the distinctive potato cakes, a sort of cookie, which were served to Watson and Sir Henry at tea. This recipe is adapted from one given in the book *Good Things in England,*[1] where it was attributed to a Mrs. Seldon. Because Mrs. Barrymore's maiden name was Selden, we infer that it originated with her or her mother. Her name was, unfortunately, misspelled either by the recipe book or (we hate to admit the possibility) by Watson.

☞ **Mrs. Barrymore's Potato Cakes**

Makes approximately 2½ dozen

2 cups mashed potatoes[2]
¾ cup melted shortening
2 cups flour
4 heaping tablespoons sugar
2 tablespoons dried currants or raisins
2 egg whites, beaten lightly
½ to 1 teaspoon salt

1) Mix the shortening and the flour.
2) Knead them together with the other ingredients.

[1] By Florence White, London: Jonathan Cape, 1932, p. 81.
[2] Instant mashed potatoes may be used, provided that they are made with only about 60 percent of the amount of liquid specified on the package. In any event, the potatoes should be as dry as possible.

3) Roll the dough out to ⅓-inch thickness and cut it into 3 to 4-inch rounds.

4) Bake them on a greased cookie sheet in a 350°F. oven for 15 to 20 minutes, or until they are light brown.

Eccles Cakes

"The Adventure of Wisteria Lodge" was brought to the attention of Holmes and Watson by way of "The Singular Adventure of Mr. John Scott Eccles." Eccles, a respectable bachelor, had accepted an invitation of a recent acquaintance to spend a few days with him at Wisteria Lodge at Esher in Surrey. After a disquieting first evening, Eccles retired to bed, and awoke the next morning to find the country house deserted. His host and his small staff of servants had all vanished completely. The solution of this mystery "covers two continents, [and] concerns two groups of mysterious persons." It is fitting to recall this adventure with a traditional English teatime treat, Eccles Cakes.

☞ Eccles Cakes

Makes approximately 2 dozen

2½ tablespoons grated orange or lemon peel
½ cup dried currants
¼ teaspoon allspice
¼ teaspoon nutmeg
4 tablespoons sugar
1 ounce butter
2 cups flour
½ teaspoon coarse salt

½ cup shortening
Water, if necessary

1) Mix the peel, currants, allspice, nutmeg, sugar, and butter in a saucepan. Heat for a few minutes, then cool and set aside.

2) Mix the flour and salt together. Work the shortening into the flour until the mixture crumbles. Add as much water as needed to make an elastic dough mixture.

3) Roll out the dough ¼-inch thick. Cut it into 3-inch rounds.

4) Place a heaping tablespoon of the cooled mixture on each round. Moisten the edges with water. Fold the edges toward the center and press them together. Flatten the cakes lightly and pierce them with a fork a few times.

5) Set them on a greased baking sheet and bake them in a 350° to 400°F. oven for 10 to 15 minutes.

Mrs. Hudson's Biscuits

Mrs. Hudson's biscuits were a staple item of food at Baker Street. They were always on hand in case of sudden need, and they were needed on at least two occasions to revive a hungry body. It was to Mrs. Hudson's biscuits that Sherlock Holmes turned to break his three-day fast in "The Adventure of the Dying Detective": Biscuits and claret, and then to Simpson's for "something nutritious." And when the imposing figure of Thorneycroft Huxtable, M.A., Ph.D., etc., collapsed from hunger and fatigue on the hearthrug at Baker Street, Mrs. Hudson's biscuits and a glass of milk brought him back to life. This was, by the way, the only occasion upon which anyone drank milk in the Canon. Perhaps abstinence from milk was wise, because in the days before pasteurization, milk was often laden either with bacteria or with formaldehyde which was added to kill the bacteria. In the light of present-day knowledge, it is hard to tell which was worse. We will presume, however, that on this occasion the milk was as wholesome as Mrs. Hudson's biscuits, which were very wholesome indeed.

☞ **Mrs. Hudson's Biscuits**

Makes about 1½ dozen

1½ teaspoons baking powder
¼ teaspoon salt
1½ cups flour
1 tablespoon butter
¾ cup milk

1) Mix together the baking powder, salt, and flour.
2) Rub in the butter with your fingers.
3) Add the milk and beat until the mixture becomes a soft dough.
4) Grease a baking pan.
5) For each biscuit, spoon out a level tablespoon of dough, and drop it on the pan, placing the biscuits 1 inch apart.
6) Bake them in a 350° to 400°F. oven for 6 to 10 minutes.

They will keep for about 1 week in a canister.

Peaches Cartwright

Cartwright was the name of the lad who brought the provisions to Holmes's solitary hut while the Great Detective investigated the legend-come-to-life of *The Hound of the Baskervilles*. Holmes himself might have eaten this dessert in an epicurean moment on the moor. The peaches came from a tin; the raspberries were gathered wild; the biscuits originated wherever it was that Cartwright obtained Holmes's bread. Instead of whipped cream, Holmes had Devonshire clotted cream, an extra-rich thick cream made chiefly in England's West country.[1] As a concession to the Spartan life, Holmes probably omitted the chocolate.

---

[1] We do not offer a recipe for Devonshire clotted cream because it must be made with extremely rich, nonhomogenized, unpasteurized milk, which is rarely available in the United States.

☞ Peaches Cartwright

Serves 10

  5 peaches or 10 peach halves (fresh, frozen, or tinned)
  10 Devonshire Splits (see recipe below)
  10 tablespoons pureed raspberries
  1 cup heavy cream
  1 teaspoon sugar
  2 to 3 drops vanilla extract
  Chocolate chips

1) Rinse the peaches and dry them. If they are fresh, peel them. Cut them in half and remove the stones.

2) Cut the Devonshire biscuits in halves and place each half, open, on a plate or in a bowl.

3) Top each biscuit with a peach half, and spoon the raspberry puree over the peaches.

4) Whip the cream with 1 teaspoon of sugar, and add 2 to 3 drops of vanilla extract. Spread it over the top of the dessert. Decorate it with chocolate chips.

DEVONSHIRE SPLITS

  1 envelope dry yeast
  2 tablespoons lukewarm water
  1 teaspoon sugar
  ¾ cup milk
  ½ teaspoon salt
  ¼ cup sweet butter
  ¼ cup sugar
  2 whole eggs, beaten
  3 egg yolks, beaten
  3 to 4 cups of flour as needed

1) Sprinkle the yeast into the lukewarm water. Add 1 teaspoon of sugar and set aside in a warm place for 5 to 10 minutes or until the mixture is foamy.

2) Scald the milk; add the salt, butter, and ¼ cup of sugar. Stir it until the butter melts. Allow it to cool to lukewarm.

3) Add it to the yeast mixture along with the beaten whole eggs and egg yolks.

4) Stir in 1 cup of flour.

5) Cover the dough loosely and set it to rise in a draught-free place for about 30 to 40 minutes, or until the dough is light and fluffy.

6) Beat in the remaining flour as needed to make the dough smooth but soft. Knead it for 10 minutes. Place it in a floured bowl; dust the top of the dough with flour; cover it loosely, and set it in a draught-free corner until it doubles in bulk, approximately 1 to 1½ hours.

7) Punch the dough down. Knead it for 2 to 3 minutes.

8) Cut off pieces about the size of an egg and roll them into balls. Dredge them lightly with flour, dusting off the excess.

9) Place them 1 inch apart on a buttered baking sheet. Allow them to rise for 30 minutes, then bake them in a preheated 300°F. oven for 1 hour, or until they are a pale golden brown.

☞

The Sideboard

The sideboard, a piece of "humble lodging house mahogany,"[1] was the center of good eating when Holmes was at home. Somehow at just the right time something tasty would appear for Mrs. Hudson's lodgers. Their habits did not allow regular mealtimes: "When will you be pleased to dine, Mr. Holmes?" Mrs. Hudson was heard to ask. "Seven-thirty the day after tomorrow," replied Holmes.[2] Far better it was for Mrs. Hudson to set a tempting meal upon the sideboard and let her lodgers eat when they were ready.

This venerable item of furniture, close to the hearts and vicarious stomachs of Sherlockians everywhere, was described most fully in an article in the *Baker Street Journal*, written with the aid of a book alleged to have belonged to Mrs. Hudson herself: " 'The panels in the back are of looking glass; and the doors of the two pedestals have panels filled with fluted silk. . . . The tops . . . are frequently formed of statuary marble, and the supports and upper shelf of finest rosewood. . . . On the bottom board, in front of the lower glass, are placed vases for holding flowers, and a number of other ornaments.' Watson and Holmes littered it with tumblers, a

[1] These were the words used by Watson to describe it in "The Adventure of the Noble Bachelor," the night when "an epicurean cold supper" was spread upon it.

[2] A colloquy reported to Watson by Billy, the page in "The Adventure of the Mazarin Stone."

cigar box, odds and ends of cold food, and of course the gasogene, and probably the tantalus."[3]

And what, the contemporary reader may ask, is a gasogene? The late Christopher Morley described it as something "which appears occasionally in English fiction and which I can only suppose to be some sort of syphon-bottle."[4] In spite of Morley's attempt to make it fictional, the object did exist. It was ably sketched by Jay Finley Christ in the *Baker Street Journal*,[5] and a contemporary collector may occasionally find an actual specimen. It is indeed a sort of syphon bottle, and it was used to provide the soda with which Holmes and Watson usually drank their whiskey.

The tantalus, an ingenious device to lock and hold whiskey bottles, is a curious matter of Sherlockian lore, for diligent searches through the Canon have failed to find any reference to one in the rooms at Baker Street.[6] It was introduced into Sherlockian legend evidently on the theory that where there is a gasogene, there must be a tantalus.

Many meals from that fabled sideboard were enjoyed by Holmes and Watson. We like to remember as typical the "forenoon . . . late in 1896" when Holmes, directing Watson to the sideboard, proposed: "Let us renew our energies before we make a fresh call upon them."[7] That day it was cold partridge on the sideboard, with a bottle of Montrachet. We suggest that a blackberry and apple pie rested beside it. A savoury salad of cheese made the meal complete.

☞ Cold Partridge, Baker Street

Serves 4

2 partridges[8]
1 ½ tablespoons cooking oil

---

[3] Paul McPharlin, "221B—Certain Physical Details," *Baker Street Journal*, 1947, 2 (old series), pp. 180–194.

[4] From the introduction to *The Complete Sherlock Holmes,* Garden City, New York: Doubleday & Co.

[5] 1946, *1* (old series), p. 69.

[6] Unlike the gasogene, which takes its place in descriptions of the Baker Street rooms (see "A Scandal in Bohemia" and "The Adventure of the Mazarin Stone"), a tantalus does not appear there. A tantalus was owned by Captain Peter Carey ("The Adventure of Black Peter"), however.

[7] This meal was one of the highlights of "The Adventure of the Veiled Lodger." Little energy was required of Holmes, whose main task, in this adventure, was to listen to Mrs. Ronder's narrative of the Abbas-Parva tragedy.

[8] A Cornish hen is an ideal substitute for the partridge in this recipe.

3 tablespoons olive oil
20 tiny white onions
2 medium-sized carrots, diced (½ pound)
½ bottle dry white wine
Juice of 1 lemon
½ cup water
1 *bouquet garni* (celery, bay leaf, parsley, chervil)
2 tomatoes, peeled, seeded, and chopped
1 tablespoon coriander seeds
5 peppercorns
1 teaspoon salt, or to taste

1) Pluck, draw, and truss the birds.

2) Heat the oil and 1 tablespoon of the olive oil in a casserole, and cook the onions and carrots to a golden brown.

3) Add the wine, lemon juice, water, *bouquet garni,* tomatoes, coriander and peppercorns. Season with salt and cook for 20 minutes.

4) Place the birds in a large casserole and pour the hot mixture over them. It should barely cover them. Simmer them, covered, for 25 minutes. Remove the *bouquet garni.*

5) Pour the birds and liquid into a deep serving dish. The liquid should just cover the birds. Sprinkle the remaining olive oil over them.

6) Chill them in the refrigerator for 6 days. Check them and turn them from time to time. If the marinade begins to bubble, pour it off and prepare a new marinade for the birds.

7) At serving time, remove the birds from the liquid. Place them on a platter and arrange the vegetables around them.

☞ A Savoury Salad of Cheddar Cheese

Serves 4

½ pound Cheddar cheese
6 olives
4 tablespoons chopped scallions
2 tablespoons vinegar[9]

---

[9] With apologies to wine connoisseurs who blanch at the thought of tasting anything with vinegar when a fine wine is at hand. Holmes and Watson, we can be sure, would have eaten the cheese from the top after the vinegar had sunk to the bottom—and advised Mrs. Hudson that when serving a salad with wine, she should at least go easy on the vinegar.

A pinch of sugar
4 to 5 grinds of pepper, or to taste
¼ cup oil

1) Cut the Cheddar cheese into cubes. Cut the olives in half.

2) Combine all ingredients but the oil. Taste. Adjust the seasonings. Add the oil.

☞ Blackberry and Apple Pie

1 to 1½ pounds large cooking apples
2 tablespoons melted butter
½ cup sugar
1 quart fresh blackberries
Short Pastry (see recipe below)
1 egg yolk mixed with 1 tablespoon sugar

1) Peel, core, and slice the apples.

2) In a heavy sauté pan, melt the butter and cook the apples over medium heat. Sprinkle them with 2 tablespoons of the sugar and stir well. The apples should not fall apart.

3) Combine the remaining sugar with the blackberries; taste them and add more sugar if necessary.

4) Spread the blackberries in a 2-inch-deep pie dish. Spoon the apples over the top.

5) Roll the pie crust dough on a floured surface. Cover the whole surface of the pie, sealing the edges with strips of dough.

6) Brush the top with the egg yolk and sugar.[10]

7) Bake for 20 to 25 minutes in a 400°F. oven, or until the dough is golden brown.

8) Cool the pie at room temperature and serve it with heavy cream.

SHORT PASTRY

Makes one 9-inch crust

1 cup flour
½ teaspoon coarse (Kosher) salt (slightly less if table salt)

---

[10] "You can tell an old master by the sweep of his brush." (Sherlock Holmes in *The Valley of Fear.*)

½ cup pork lard or shortening
Water as needed

1) Mix the flour and the salt. Work the shortening into the flour until the mixture becomes crumbly.

2) Add as much water as is needed to make an elastic dough mixture.

"Dr. Watson, Mr. Sherlock Holmes"

"Dr. Watson, Mr. Sherlock Holmes." These were the words of young Stamford as he introduced Sherlock Holmes and John H. Watson, M.D., to each other at the chemical laboratory at Bart's (St. Bartholomew's Hospital in London) in 1881. This simple phrase provoked the now famous reply from Sherlock Holmes, "How are you? You have been in Afghanistan, I perceive." Both doctor and Detective had hoped to find someone with whom to share lodgings, and it was young Stamford, their mutual acquaintance, who had brought them together. The beginning of the long friendship is described in *A Study in Scarlet*.

In briefly exploring their mutual compatibility, Holmes listed his tobacco, chemical experiments, and virtuosity with the violin among those traits which might annoy a fellow boarder. In addition, he admitted, "I get in the dumps at times, and don't open my mouth for days on end." As for Watson, he confessed, "I keep a bull pup,[1] and I object to row because my nerves are shaken, and I get up at all sorts of ungodly hours, and I am extremely lazy." To further arouse the curiosity of readers through the ages, the doctor added, "I have another set of vices when I'm well, but those are the principal ones at present." Generations of devotees have since

---

[1] Which raises the image of a dog's lapping up the sideboard's leftovers, but curiously, the bull pup is never mentioned again. Did the dog meet some unfortunate end at the hands of Holmes, Mrs. Hudson, or Watson himself? Did the dog remain at Baker Street, unmentioned? Was the dog fictional from the beginning? Or was "bull pup" colloquial for one of Watson's old army weapons? Each of these possibilities has been championed by one critic or another. For a full account, see Ronald DeWaal, *World Bibliography of Sherlock Holmes and Dr. Watson*, Boston: New York Graphic Society, 1974, p. 212.

speculated upon those vices, but Watson did not see fit to publicize them in later adventures.[2]

Having given what each believed to be a fair account of his own short-comings, neither communicated much to the other about his own affairs. Holmes, with his insatiable curiosity, must have taken an interest in the private life of his fellow boarder, but as a gentleman, and not suspecting Watson of any crime, he did not investigate. We are certain, however, that before long he had deduced a great deal about his roommate's past and present.

Because Dr. Watson was the chronicler, we know more of his own first impressions of his future friend. Like Holmes, Watson maintained a gentlemanly respect for his companion's privacy. But, with appropriate apologies, he jotted down a curious list of traits, concluding, for example, that Holmes had no knowledge at all of philosophy, astronomy, and literature, other than the sensational.

These first impressions did not always prove accurate. Watson's errors may be put down to his human frailty in drawing quick conclusions, but they are very largely Holmes's fault as well. The Master had a habit of pulling his companion's leg by making exaggerated statements about himself.

And Mrs. Hudson? What would her list have looked like? What did she think of her new boarders? Of Holmes's rambles through London? Of Watson's sedentary ways? Of the strange parade of visitors? A pity it is that no one was at her side to chronicle her reaction to the first-floor tenants.[3] Landladies do not always tolerate eccentricity when more conventional lodgers might be had. The world will never know how long it was before her attitude turned to understanding and her understanding to devotion. But it can be grateful.

We suspect that at the time of this first adventure, *A Study in Scarlet*, Mrs. Hudson did not yet know how unpredictable the Detective's appetite was to be, and that she planned hot dishes to be served at regular hours. Holmes, in this adventure, appears to have obliged her meal plans.

Holmes was uniquely able to disengage himself from whatever he was doing and to focus his attentions elsewhere with equal single-mindedness. He had lunch and then took time out for entertainment. "And now for lunch, and then for Norman Neruda.[4] Her attack and her bowing are

---

[2] Although we have little specific evidence, the few clues that we have been given point to women and gambling. On the subject of women, Watson once boasted of "experience of women which extends over many nations and three separate continents" (*The Sign of Four*). With respect to gambling, he once confessed, "I pay for [horse racing] with about half my wound pension" ("The Adventure of Shoscombe Old Place").

[3] In the United States, Holmes and Watson would have been "second-floor" tenants, but in England, "first-floor" refers to the first story above the ground floor.

[4] Referring to the noted violin virtuoso Mme. Norman-Neruda, or Lady Hallé.

splendid. What's that little thing of Chopin's that she plays so magnificently: Tra-la-la-lira-lira-lay." Sherlock Holmes engaged in some postconcert sleuthing and returned when dinner was on the table.

A BAKER STREET LUNCHEON

Stuffed Lemon Piquant
Roast Chicken Lestrade
Spinach Tarts

A BAKER STREET DINNER

Clear Oxtail Soup
Braised Spring Lamb
Stuffed Tomato
Almond Pudding
Marrow Toast

☞ **Stuffed Lemon Piquant**[5]

Serves 8

4 lemons
2 cans of sardines (7 to 8 oz.)
4 tablespoons mayonnaise
2 tablespoons tomato catsup
1 teaspoon sweet paprika
Salt only if needed; start with $\frac{1}{3}$ teaspoon
3 grinds white pepper
4 stuffed Spanish olives
2 tablespoons pimiento strips
8 large lettuce leaves

---

[5] To honour Watson's reaction when he first met Holmes. He remarked to Stamford: "This is very piquant. I am much obliged to you for bringing us together."

1) Wash the lemons, dry them, and cut them in half lengthwise.

2) Remove the pulp with a grapefruit knife. Reserve the shells.

3) Remove the pips[6] (seeds) and the celluloid skin, and dice the pulp small.

4) Drain the sardines and puree them with a fork. Add them to the lemon pulp.

5) Mix the mayonnaise and tomato catsup together. Fold it into the sardines and lemon pulp. Season with paprika, salt, and pepper.

6) Fill the lemon shells with the mixture and garnish each one with half a stuffed olive and a pimiento strip.

7) Cool them for 30 minutes and serve them on salad leaves.

☞ Roast Chicken Lestrade[7]

Serves 4

1 rooster (2 pounds)
1/3 to 1/2 teaspoon salt, or to taste
4 strips bacon (2 1/2 ounces)
1 small onion (1 1/2 ounces)
6 to 8 new potatoes or small potatoes (1/2 pound)
3 ounces canned mushrooms
2 ounces green olives without stones
1 tablespoon oil
3 to 4 grinds black pepper, or to taste
1 pinch garlic salt
1 tablespoon brandy[8]
8 cherry tomatoes or 3 small tomatoes (7 ounces in all)

1) Rinse the rooster well, dry it with a towel, and season it with salt inside and outside.

2) Cut the bacon into small dice.

3) Peel the onion and dice it coarsely.

4) Peel the potatoes; wash and drain them.

---

[6] You may reserve the lemon pips as a substitute for orange pips in threatening letters to used hansom dealers.

[7] This dish was given its name over lunch, we fancy, when Holmes and Watson recalled Inspector Lestrade's comment earlier that day: "This case will make a stir, sir. It beats anything I have seen, and I am no chicken."

[8] Brandy recalls a later incident in Inspector Lestrade's career: when he offered the beverage to Sir Henry Baskerville in the fog of Dartmoor after the Baskerville heir had been savagely attacked by the all-too-corporeal legendary hound.

5) Drain the mushrooms and olives.

6) Heat the oil in a roasting pan and sauté the bacon for 5 minutes.

7) Add the onions and sauté them lightly until they are transparent.

8) Add the potatoes and brown them lightly.

9) Add the olives, mushrooms, salt, pepper, and garlic salt.

10) Set the rooster, breast up, in the roasting pan with the vegetables.

11) Pour the brandy over the chicken.

12) Cover it and roast it in a preheated oven at 350° to 375°F. for 90 minutes. Turn the rooster after 45 minutes, and if more colour is desired, remove the cover during the last 15 minutes of cooking.

13) Cut the cherry tomatoes in half or the tomatoes into wedges, and add them to the pan for the last 10 minutes of cooking.

14) Remove the pan from the oven. Taste the contents and adjust the seasoning.

☞ Spinach Tarts

Serves 4

½ cup flour
3 tablespoons oil
A pinch of salt
½ cup water
1 pound fresh or 6 ounces frozen spinach
2 cups water
⅓ teaspoon salt, or to taste
1 ounce butter
½ pound lean cottage cheese
1 heaping tablespoon grated Parmesan cheese
4 small eggs
2 tablespoons oil to brush the tarts

1) Mix the flour, 3 tablespoons oil, salt, and water to a smooth dough.

2) Cover and allow it to rest in the refrigerator for 1 hour.

3) Clean the spinach, and simmer it in 2 cups of boiling salted water for 10 minutes. (If using frozen spinach, prepare it according to the package directions.)

4) Drain it, and puree it in a blender or grind it through a fine blade.

5) Heat the butter and pureed spinach and sauté for 3 minutes.

6) Puree the cottage cheese in a blender and mix it in a bowl with the spinach. Add ¾ of the Parmesan cheese and mix well.

7) Divide the dough into 8 equal pieces and roll them out.

8) Oil 4 small pie dishes and line each one with 1 piece of dough.

9) Spread the spinach stuffing over each of the 4 pieces of dough.

10) Press a hole into each of the spinach fillings, and break 1 egg into each of them. Sprinkle them with the rest of the Parmesan cheese.

11) Top them with the 4 remaining pieces of dough.

12) Pierce the top of each pie a few times to allow the steam to escape, and brush the tops with oil. Bake them in a preheated 280° to 325°F. oven for 60 minutes.

The tarts may be served either hot or cold.

☞ Clear Oxtail Soup

Serves 4

1 whole oxtail
Water
1 to 2 teaspoons salt, or to taste
2 carrots
4 onions
½ celeriac root (knob celery)
1 parsnip
3 cloves of garlic
⅓ teaspoon thyme
½ teaspoon mace
8 peppercorns
4 tablespoons oil or lard
1½ ounces brandy or white wine

1) Cut the oxtail into small pieces at the joints.

2) Boil the meat for 5 to 10 minutes in salted water. Remove the pieces from the water and dry them.

3) Dice the carrots, onions, celery, and parsnip.

4) Tie all the herbs in a cheesecloth.

5) Heat the oil. Brown the oxtail. Add the vegetables, and sauté them for 5 minutes.

6) Cover the oxtail and vegetables well with water. Add the herbs, and simmer uncovered until the meat loosens from the bone (about 1½ hours). Skim the soup.

7) Strain the broth through a cheesecloth. Remove all meat from the bones and add it to the soup. Adjust the seasoning.

8) Before serving, add a small amount of brandy or white wine (approximately 1 to 2 tablespoons).

☞ **Braised Spring Lamb**

Serves 4

1½ to 2 pounds cooked meat from a leg of lamb
½ to 1 teaspoon crushed black peppercorns, or to taste
2½ ounces butter
1 to 1½ teaspoons salt
1 large onion (6 ounces)
1 cup hot water

1) Cut the meat into 4 portions.

2) Rub the meat with crushed pepper.

3) Heat the butter in a large pot and brown the meat for 10 minutes on each side. Add salt.

4) Slice the onion. Remove the meat from the pot and sauté the onion for 5 minutes. Return the meat to the pot and add the water. Taste it and adjust the seasoning.

5) Simmer it covered for 30 minutes. Serve it very hot.

☞ **Stuffed Tomato**

Serves 4

2 stale hard rolls
2 small cloves of garlic
⅓ to ½ teaspoon salt, or to taste
2 eggs
4 ounces butter
2 to 3 grinds black pepper, or to taste
4 tomatoes (12 ounces)
4 sprigs of parsley

1) Soak the rolls for 5 minutes in water to cover.

2) Peel the garlic and crush with salt to a fine paste.

3) Squeeze the water out of the rolls and cut them into small pieces.

4) Add the garlic paste, eggs, and 3 ounces of butter to the bread pieces and work into a smooth dough. Season with salt and pepper.

5) Wash the tomatoes and dry them. Remove the stems and cut off the top third of the tomatoes. Save the tops.

6) Carefully scoop out the lower two-thirds of the tomatoes, and salt them slightly.

7) Stuff the tomatoes with the bread mixture. Top them with the tomato covers, and set them into a greased fireproof dish.

8) Melt 1 ounce of the butter and sprinkle it over the tomatoes.

9) Bake for 15 minutes at 350°F.

10) Garnish with parsley.

☞ Almond Pudding

Serves 4

3½ ounces butter
4 heaping tablespoons sugar
2 teaspoons vanilla sugar (1 package)[9]
6 eggs, separated
3½ ounces grated almonds

1) Whip the butter, sugar, vanilla sugar, and egg yolks with an electric mixer until they are creamy.

2) Fold the grated almonds carefully into this mixture.

3) Set the mixture over hot water in a double boiler and whisk it until it is a thick, creamy consistency.

4) Whip the egg whites into a meringue, and fold them into the mixture in the double boiler.

5) Grease a pudding mould or a 1- to 1½-quart casserole with butter. Fill it with the pudding mixture. Cover it with a lid or aluminum foil, and set it on a trivet in a pan of water. The water should reach three-fourths of the way up the side of the mould. Bring the water to a boil. Cook the pudding over the simmering water for 40 minutes, replenishing the water if necessary.

6) Remove the mould and rinse it under cold water for 1 minute.

7) Open the mould and allow the steam to escape for 2 minutes.

8) Turn it onto a plate and serve it immediately with Vanilla Sauce (see recipe following).

---

[9] As a substitute, use 2 to 3 drops of vanilla extract and increase the sugar by 2 teaspoons.

VANILLA SAUCE

Serves 4

2 cups milk
3 egg yolks
3 tablespoons sugar
1 teaspoon cornstarch
4 drops vanilla extract (or more if a strong vanilla flavor is desired)

1) Heat the milk.
2) Mix the egg yolks, sugar, and cornstarch in a bowl.
3) Add them to the milk. Beat the ingredients in the top of a double boiler over heat until they are thick.
4) Add the vanilla to taste.

☞ Marrow Toast

Serves 4

4 two-inch center sections of marrowbone
4 slices of bread, toasted
A pinch of salt
2 grinds of black pepper for each slice of toast
Lemon juice to taste
Freshly chopped chives

1) Have the butcher cut about four 2-inch sections of marrow bone.
2) Push the marrow out of the bone and soak it in cold water for 30 minutes or overnight.
3) Slice the marrow and place it on the slices of toast. Season it with salt, freshly ground black pepper, and lemon juice. Put it under the broiler until the marrow has melted. Sprinkle some freshly chopped chives on top of it, and serve it hot.

Note: The bones may be used for a good beef broth.

"Oysters, and a brace of grouse, with something a little choice in white wines"

Holmes's "merits as a housekeeper" came to the fore during *The Sign of Four.* After sleuthing all day disguised as a seafarer, he returned to Baker Street to dazzle Dr. Watson and detective Athelney Jones not only with his deductions, but also with his meal preparations: "It will be ready in half an hour. I have oysters and a brace of grouse with something a little choice in white wines." His very willingness to consider dining indicated that the mystery was all but solved.

Characteristically, Holmes's companions had to wait until the table had been cleared and three glasses filled with port before they learned of Holmes's successful exploits. Meanwhile, Holmes regaled them with a cheerful discussion "on a quick succession of subjects—on miracle plays, on medieval pottery, on Stradivarius violins, on the Buddhism of Ceylon, and on the warships of the future—handling each as though he had made a special study of it."

It must be accepted that Holmes was responsible for the meal, because he referred to himself as "housekeeper." Why Mrs. Hudson had the night off, no one will ever know. But having been occupied with his investigation all day, Holmes could not have done much in advance of his return. His ability to plan a meal that was to be ready so quickly was amazing. But "every problem becomes very childish once it is explained,"[1] and the meal preparation was simplicity itself.

Holmes merely stopped at a shop on his way home and purchased the grouse already cooked.

[1] "The Adventure of the Dancing Men."

Curiously, one brace of grouse (2 birds) would scarcely suffice for three hungry men. One critic[2] has suggested that (Watson's memory having failed) three brace of grouse were served. This is plausible, but no more so than the grouse's being just one among other cold meats bought on the way home. The final touches could be added in no more than 30 minutes. We offer, therefore, the following menu:

> Oyster Cocktail
> Cold Roast Grouse with Cold Cuts
> Fresh Grapes
> Cold Horseradish Sauce
> Toast with Butter
> Stilton Cheese
> Port Wine

☞ Oyster Cocktail

Serves 4

2 to 3 tablespoons mayonnaise
1 tablespoon grated fresh horseradish or
    ½ tablespoon prepared horseradish
3 tablespoons tomato catsup
A little lemon juice
1 teaspoon Worcestershire sauce
5 drops tabasco sauce (optional)
⅓ teaspoon salt, or to taste
1 to 2 pinches of sugar
A pinch of ginger
20 oysters[3]
2 sprigs of parsley

1) Mix together the mayonnaise, horseradish, catsup, lemon juice, Worcestershire sauce, tabasco sauce, salt, sugar, and ginger.

2) Remove the oysters from their shells. Add 16 oysters to the above mixture. Mix together well, and allow to rest for 15 minutes.

3) Pour into 4 champagne glasses. Adjust the seasoning to taste, and garnish each dish with 1 oyster and some parsley.

With this dish, English gourmets usually prefer a mixture of light and dark beer. A Frenchman would usually accompany it with champagne or

[2] Fletcher Pratt, "The Gastronomic Holmes," *Baker Street Journal,* 1952, 2, pp. 94–99.
[3] Smoked or pickled oysters may be substituted for the fresh oysters in this recipe.

chablis. Holmes's choice of white wine on this occasion may reflect his French ancestry. He was, as we know, a descendant on his mother's side of the artist Vernet.[4]

☞ Cold Roast Grouse with Cold Cuts

Serves 4

1 brace of grouse (2 grouse)
3½ ounces cold roast veal
3½ ounces cold roast smoked loin of pork
3½ ounces cold canned ham
2 tomatoes, cut into wedges
2 hard-boiled eggs, halved
Parsley for garnish

1) Prepare the brace of grouse according to the recipe for Grouse English Style, which follows. Carve them according to the instructions for Cold Roast Pheasant, p. 114. Chill them.

2) Buy the other cold cuts at a delicatessen.

3) Arrange the cold meat in a twirl on a large tray.

4) Decorate the arrangement with the tomato wedges, egg halves, and parsley.

Serve it with fresh grapes, horseradish sauce, and toast with butter.

☞ Brace of Grouse—English Style

Serves 4

4 oven-ready grouse or partridge, 8 to 10 ounces each[5]
2 teaspoons salt, or to taste
½ teaspoon pepper, or to taste
4 strips bacon
2 ounces margarine or butter
1 cup hot water

[4] From his revelation in "The Greek Interpreter."

[5] Cornish hen or squab may be substituted. The more educated palates, those accustomed to the flavour of wild game, will detect the difference, but the recipe will be delicious nonetheless.

1) Rinse the grouse well and dry them. Season with salt and pepper. Bard them with bacon by pinning pieces of bacon to the birds with toothpicks.

2) Heat the margarine or butter in a large skillet and sauté the grouse for 5 minutes on all sides.

3) Add the hot water and braise them for 30 minutes.

4) When the birds are cooked, remove the toothpicks and bacon.

☞ Cold Horseradish Sauce

Makes 3–4 cups

1 cup heavy cream
3 ounces grated horseradish (fresh or frozen)
Salt to taste
$1/3$ teaspoon sugar
$1/3$ teaspoon black pepper

Whip the heavy cream and mix it with the grated horseradish, salt, sugar, and pepper.

After Tea on a Summer Evening, or Enter Mycroft

Of all the men who appear in the Writings, few have captured the imagination of the devotees of Holmesiana as has Mycroft Holmes, Sherlock's brother.[1] Mycroft, mentioned seldom in the stories, appears personally in three vignettes which serve only to tantalize the reader.[2]

[1] We cannot say this without mentioning, at least in passing, the late unlamented Professor Moriarty, who, like Mycroft, is mentioned by name in few of the stories, and who has also become magnified in legend.

[2] The stories in which Mycroft appears are "The Greek Interpreter," during which Dr. Watson met Mycroft Holmes for the first time; "The Adventure of the Bruce-Partington Plans"; and "The Final Problem," in which he appears briefly as a coachman.

Watson had a "long and intimate acquaintance" with Holmes before the Master revealed anything at all about his own family.[3] So reticent was Holmes that Watson had come to believe that he "was an orphan with no relatives living." In "The Greek Interpreter," during a moment of relaxation in their rooms at Baker Street—"It was after tea on a summer evening"—Holmes was moved to speak of his history: "My ancestors were country squires, who appear to have led much the same life as is natural to their class. But . . . my grandmother . . . was the sister of Vernet, the French artist." And, to the great surprise of Watson, Holmes had a living brother, Mycroft. And to his even greater surprise, Holmes offered to introduce him that very night.

Mycroft, so we are told, was superior to Sherlock in powers of observation and deduction but could never rival the Master as a detective, because he loathed all forms of physical activity, which might well have accounted for another of Mycroft's most notable characteristics: his corpulent physique. There is no evidence that Mycroft had given his life over to food, or that he enjoyed stuffing himself at the multi-course banquets associated with his era. On the contrary, it is improbable that Mycroft would have attended any social function at all.

Sharing with Sherlock a distaste for the limelight, and lacking a chronicler like Watson, Mycroft was virtually unknown outside his own circle, which was the Diogenes Club, a club for the unsociable among men. Mycroft Holmes lodged in Pall Mall just opposite the Diogenes Club: "His Pall Mall lodgings, the Diogenes Club, Whitehall—that is his cycle." To deviate from this was virtually unknown: "A planet might as well leave its orbit." It is therefore more than likely that his obesity was the result of a singular lack of exercise.

How did this extraordinary man make a living? At first introduction, that is, in "The Greek Interpreter," Holmes explained to Watson that Mycroft "has an extraordinary faculty for figures, and audits the books in some of the government departments," but this disclosure was incomplete. Holmes later apologized during "The Adventure of the Bruce-Partington Plans" and revealed the true importance of Mycroft ("I did not know you quite so well in those days," Holmes explained). Mycroft was not just a minor functionary in the British Government, Holmes said; "You would . . . be right in a sense if you said that occasionally he is the British Government."

This is the brother whom Watson met on that summer evening which had begun so unremarkably with tea. As part of a most remarkable evening, however, it can never be forgotten.

---

[3] Watson was reticent about his own affairs as well. It was not until about the same time, so the Canon leads us to believe, that Holmes knew anything about his own good friend's brother, and then only by deducing the late brother and his problems from Watson's newly inherited watch. (*The Sign of Four.*)

A SUMMER'S BAKER STREET TEA

Cucumber Sandwiches
Sally Lunn Bread
Tea

☞ **Cucumber Sandwiches**

8 tea sandwiches

3 sardines
¼ pound butter
4 slices white bread or Sally Lunn bread
10 slices of cucumber
8 black olives

1) Blend the sardines and butter together, using a blender or a sieve, to make sardine butter.

2) Spread 1 ounce of sardine butter over each slice of bread. Top 2 slices with the cucumber and top each of these slices with the remaining 2 slices. Cut each sandwich into 4 triangles. Decorate each triangle with an olive, secured by a toothpick. Serve them on a plate garnished with watercress or mustardcress.

☞ **Sally Lunn Bread**

1 loaf

3 egg yolks
2 egg whites
1 ounce fresh compressed yeast
A pinch of sugar
1 cup heavy cream or evaporated milk (at room temperature)
A pinch of salt
4 cups flour
A few tablespoons warm water

1) Beat the egg yolks and whites.
2) Cream the yeast with a pinch of sugar.

3) Whisk the eggs, cream (at room temperature), and the yeast together. Add a pinch of salt.

4) Put the flour in a large bowl. Add the liquid ingredients. Mix them together, adding just enough warm water (1 tablespoon at a time) to lightly wet the flour.

5) Set the dough aside in a warm place to rise until it doubles in bulk, about 1½ hours.

6) Knead the dough for about 5 minutes, or until it is no longer sticky.

7) Form it into a loaf and put it aside to rise again before baking it.

8) Bake it in a preheated 350° to 400°F. oven for approximately 30 minutes.

9) It was customary to break the bread open horizontally, butter it, and return it to the oven briefly while the butter melted.

The Irregular Sandwich

Sherlock Holmes usually reserved mealtime as a period of relaxation. If he was in the middle of a case, he suspended all discussion of it until after the last course had been enjoyed. Occasionally, however, he departed from custom and took a sandwich as he worked on a problem. When Holmes prepared his own sandwich, it must of necessity have been "simplicity itself." Watson has described the most Canonical sandwich of all, made by Holmes as he set out for an afternoon of serious investigation in "The Adventure of the Beryl Coronet":

"He cut a slice of beef from the joint on the sideboard, sandwiched it between two rounds of bread, and thrusting this rude meal into his pocket, he started off upon his expedition."

The beef on the sideboard, we suggest, was cold roast beef, English style; the bread was white bread.

☞ Roast Beef—English Style

> 1 shellstrip of beef
> 2 teaspoons coarse salt

¾ teaspoon crushed black peppercorns
⅓ teaspoon thyme
⅓ teaspoon allspice
1 clove garlic, crushed
⅓ teaspoon crushed bay leaf
⅓ teaspoon MSG (optional)

1) Mix the seasonings and rub them into the shellstrip of beef. Let it cure for 24 hours.

2) Roast the meat in a 325° to 350°F. oven for about 15 to 20 minutes per pound, or until the meat is medium-rare or 150° to 160° on a meat thermometer.

3) Serve hot or cold.

☞ White Bread

1 loaf

4½ cups flour
1½ ounces fresh compressed yeast
1 teaspoon sugar
1½ to 2 cups milk
1½ ounces butter
½ teaspoon salt

1) Put the flour into a large bowl. Press a well into the centre of the flour.

2) Flake the yeast into the centre of the well. Add the sugar and a little of the milk. Mix the centre ingredients with a little of the adjacent flour to make a light, somewhat watery dough.

3) Cover the bowl with a towel and allow it to rest for 30 minutes.

4) Add the rest of the milk, the butter in small flakes, and the salt. Gradually work in the flour, starting in the centre, and proceeding outward in a spiral motion until it is all mixed.

5) Knead the dough until it forms blisters under the surface. Throw the dough hard against the side of the bowl to remove any air that may be trapped inside.

6) Cover the bowl with a towel, and allow the dough to rise for 30 minutes, or until it has doubled in bulk.

7) Form the dough into a long loaf. Set it on a greased baking pan, or in a loaf pan. Allow it to rise, covered, for 10 to 15 minutes. Brush the top of the loaf with water.

8) Bake it in a preheated oven at 300° to 350°F. for 60 minutes.

9) Remove the bread from the oven and, while it is hot, brush it with milk. Allow it to cool.

Note: Caraway seeds (1 to 2 teaspoons) may be sprinkled over the bread before baking it.

Nowhere is the sandwich-eating Holmes more evident than in "The Adventure of the Second Stain." The Great Detective was called upon by the Secretary of European Affairs, the Right Honourable Trelawney Hope, to recover a document of immense national importance. The case was extremely complex, with many clues and many more false leads. Even so, Holmes began it optimistically: "Do you stay on guard, my good Watson, and receive any fresh visitors. I'll join you at lunch if I am able."

The initial optimism was soon disappointed. Not only did Holmes not return for lunch, he slipped into "a mood which his friends would call taciturn, and others morose. He ran out and in, smoked incessantly, played snatches on his violin, sank into reveries, devoured sandwiches at irregular intervals, and hardly answered the casual questions which [Watson] put to him."

He ate only the irregular sandwiches for three days, until he was on the brink of solving the case. On the fourth morning, Watson met him at breakfast. Of all the irregular sandwiches, one is easy to deduce: the herring sandwich. We specify Bismarck herring in the recipe because of the international implications of this case, but any sort of herring may be used. We must note, however, that Sherlock Holmes always tried to avoid red ones.

☞ Herring Sandwich

Makes 4 open-faced sandwiches

4 fillets Bismarck herring
4 rings from a medium-sized onion
2 hard-cooked eggs
4 slices white bread, toasted or plain
4 lettuce leaves
1 teaspoon chopped dill

1) Cut the herring into small pieces and slice the eggs.

2) Butter the bread or toast and top it with lettuce. Top the lettuce with the herring, and garnish it with the onion rings, hard-cooked egg slices, and chopped dill.

Enter Mrs. Turner

Mrs. Hudson, the ever faithful landlady at 221B Baker Street, is almost as familiar to the devotees of the Canon as are Holmes and Watson themselves. Mysteriously, in "A Scandal in Bohemia," a new landlady appears, bearing the tray of "the simple fare our landlady has provided us." It is Mrs. Turner, who is as mysterious in her own way as is "the late Irene Adler, of dubious and questionable memory," who makes her debut in the same story. In referring to Mrs. Turner, could it be that Sherlock Holmes had forgotten the name of his landlady? That is rather unlikely for a man of his attention to minutiae.[1]

Several identities have been bestowed upon the elusive Mrs. Turner by the various critics: She may have been Jennie Turner, widow of Mrs. Hudson's cousin, Jack Turner, who "took care of things for a fortnight" while Mrs. Hudson "was in Brighton for a breath of air."[2] She may actually have been Mrs. Hudson under another name, having had a brief, unsuccessful marriage to a man named Turner.[3] Or the name Turner may have been the alias taken by Holmes and Mrs. Hudson while they (how audacious a suggestion) had been away together as lovers. The "Mrs. Turner," under that hypothesis, was but a slip of the tongue.[4]

In another speculation, Mrs. Turner was purported to be the sister of Professor Moriarty. She was sent by her brother to learn where it was that

[1] Vincent Starrett made the slightly more plausible suggestion that it was not Holmes but Dr. Watson who erred, that is, when he committed "A Scandal in Bohemia" to writing. ("The Singular Adventures of Martha Hudson," in *The Private Life of Sherlock Holmes*, Chicago: University of Chicago Press, 1960.) We reject this notion as unlikely, for surely an error as gross as this, if made at all, would be detected upon proofreading.

[2] Russell McLauchlin, "Mrs. Hudson speaks," *Baker Street Journal*, 1947, 2 (old series), pp. 329–331. Recorded by Miss ZaSu Pitts for the Amateur Mendicant Society of Detroit, March 14, 1947.

[3] Lenore Glen Offord, "The Brief Adventure of Mrs. Turner," *Baker Street Journal*, 1946, *1* (old series) pp. 253–259.

[4] Manly Wade Wellman, "The Great Man's Great Son," *Baker Street Journal*, 1946, *1* (old series), pp. 326–336. The issue of this relationship is said to be Jeeves, valet to Bertie Wooster in the writings of P. G. Wodehouse.

Dr. Watson got his material for his stories. She was astonished to learn that Sherlock Holmes really existed.[5]

Finally, Mrs. Turner may have been, not another landlady, but (how simple and prosaic a possibility) the *maid* at 221B. Merely because the landlady (Mrs. Hudson, of course) had provided the food, she need not have served it. A maid had been referred to in other stories but never, unless in this one, by name.[6]

Whatever the identity of the tray bearer, the nature of "the simple fare" remains beyond dispute. It was cold beef and beer. Appropriate embellishments, of course, accompanied it.

Roast Beef Mrs. Turner
Rye Bread
Salted Black Radish
Beer

☞ Roast Beef Mrs. Turner

Serves 4

12 slices medium-rare roast beef (see recipe, p. 100)
½ cup mayonnaise
2 teaspoons pickle relish
12 1½-inch sticks of celery

Mix the mayonnaise with the pickle relish and spread it thinly over the beef slices. Top each slice with a celery stick, and roll it into a roulade.

☞ Rye Bread

1 loaf

1 package dry yeast
½ cup lukewarm water
1 tablespoon brown sugar
⅓ cup molasses
1¼ cups boiling water
2 tablespoons butter

[5] L. A. Morrow, "More Letters from Somewhere," *Baker Street Journal*, 1968, *18*, pp. 144–146. This argument does not hold water, however, for it is based on 221B's being Watson's residence at that time. The good doctor was married and living elsewhere during "A Scandal in Bohemia."

[6] Robert R. Pattrick, "The Case of the Superfluous Landlady," *Baker Street Journal*, 1953, *3* (new series), pp. 241–243.

1 tablespoon salt
½ cup buckwheat flour
1 cup whole-wheat flour
2 cups rye flour

(This bread may be made with 3 cups rye flour and ½ cup buckwheat flour, or with 2½ cups rye flour and 1 cup whole-wheat flour, instead of the above combination of three flours. The three-flour formula, however, gives the best result.)

1) Combine the yeast, lukewarm water, brown sugar, and molasses in a bowl. Let it rest until it becomes frothy.

2) Add the boiling water to the butter and salt. Let it cool until it becomes lukewarm, and add it to the yeast mixture.

3) Combine the flours in a large bowl, and pour in the yeast-water mixture. Beat it vigorously. Flours differ in moisture content, so it may be necessary to adjust the amount of water. Lukewarm water may be added, 1 tablespoon at a time, in order to make a dough that is resilient and not too soft. Be careful not to add too much water.

4) Beat the dough for 2 to 3 minutes.

5) Set the bowl in a large pan of *hot* water. Cover it with a towel, and let the dough rise for about 1 hour. It should double in size and become light.

6) Beat the dough for 3 minutes. (If, after the previous rising period, the dough is difficult to beat, up to 2 tablespoons of warm water may be added in order to bring it to a light, spongy consistency.)

7) After beating it, put the dough into an oiled 3 by 5½ by 9¼-inch bread pan. Set the pan in warm water. Cover it with a towel, and let the dough rise again for 45 minutes. The dough at this point should be rounding over the top of the pan. Put it into a cold oven and set the temperature at 400°F. to complete the rising. After 10 to 15 minutes (as soon as the oven reaches 400°), turn the heat down to 325° and bake it for 40 minutes more. Turn the bread out onto a bread board and cover it loosely while it cools.

Note: If the bread sinks in the center or cracks open, one of two things has gone wrong: either the bread was not beaten properly, or too much liquid was added.

☞ Salted Black Radish

Serves 4

4 black radishes
3 teaspoons coarse (Kosher) salt

Peel the radishes and rinse them well. Cut them with a radish cutter, or if no radish cutter is available, cut the radishes in half, and starting on the outside of the radish, cut each one into very thin slices, about three-fourths of the way through. The slices should hold together.

Salt the radish between the slices, and allow it to rest for 20 minutes. By that time the radish should be very watery.

A Cold Supper for Burglars

Was Sherlock Holmes a criminal? Shocking as this suggestion may be, the evidence points to a chronic disregard for the letter of the law. At no time is this so blatant as the winter night on which the viands on the sideboard nourished Holmes and Watson as they prepared to commit a burglary.[1] Their cause was just, but their actions were a crime, nonetheless. Charles Augustus Milverton, the blackmailer, had victimized London society long enough to suit Holmes. The nefarious actions of "the worst man in London" could be stopped only through drastic action. Holmes gained knowledge of the premises by falsely wooing Milverton's housemaid, Agatha (blushes, Holmes!), and designed to break into the villain's house to confiscate once and for all those compromising documents through which this cunning man was extorting a huge sum of money from a client of Holmes. Faithful Watson insisted on joining his friend in this daring venture. Consenting, the detective remarked, "We have shared this same room for some years, and it would be amusing if we ended by sharing the same cell. You know, Watson, I don't mind confessing to you that I have always had an idea that I would have made a highly efficient criminal. This is the chance of my lifetime in that direction." Before embarking, they sought nourishment. Suggested Holmes, "We shall have some cold supper before we start."

The willingness of Holmes and Watson to take the law into their own hands can be seen throughout the Canon. In one of the earliest adventures, "A Scandal in Bohemia," they both agree on that point:

[1] In "The Adventure of Charles Augustus Milverton."

Holmes: "You don't mind breaking the law?"

Watson: "Not in the least."

Holmes: "Nor running a chance of arrest?"

Watson: "Not in a good cause."

Nor did Holmes blanch at being called a burglar. When, in "The Disappearance of Lady Frances Carfax," his antagonist derided, "Why, you are a common burglar," Holmes replied, "So you might describe me. . . . My companion is also a dangerous ruffian."

Those who love Sherlock Holmes, however, cannot dismiss the criminal label so lightly. For example, S. Tupper Bigelow[2] went through great legal convolutions to prove that no felony was committed in any of the cases in which the Master was reputed to have resorted to criminal means. In the case of the Milverton burglary, Magistrate Bigelow insisted that when our beloved pair broke into the blackmailer's dwelling, there was no criminal intent—only the intent to do malicious mischief—"a misdemeanour, not a felony." Only one well schooled in law could attempt so technical a defense in so incriminating a situation. Were Holmes and Watson burglars? We leave that for the jury of readers to deliberate over supper.

Let us return then to that cold supper from the sideboard at Baker Street. Surely, Holmes must have rung the bell for two bowls of hot soup for warmth on a cold night. Following the soup, cold roast pork would be in order. The menu follows:

> Lentil Soup
> Roast Loin of Pork with Apple Sauce
> English Dill Loaf
> Gingerbread

☞ Lentil Soup

Serves 4 to 5

5 to 6 ounces lentils
2 strips bacon ($\frac{1}{2}$ ounce)
1 ounce butter
$\frac{1}{2}$ cup carrots, diced small
$\frac{1}{3}$ cup onions, diced small
$\frac{1}{3}$ cup celery, diced small
2 tablespoons leek, diced small

[2] "Sherlock Holmes Was No Burglar," in *Baker Street Journal Christmas Annual,* 1958, pp. 26–37.

1 tablespoon distilled white vinegar
⅓ teaspoon salt, if necessary
2 to 3 grinds of black pepper
3 cups beef stock (canned or homemade, or from bouillon cubes)
3 peppercorns
2 to 3 pinches of oregano
2 to 3 frankfurters, diced
2 to 3 dashes Worcestershire sauce

1) Bring the lentils to one boil in water. Rinse and drain them.

2) Dice the bacon and melt it with the butter in a soup pot.

3) Add the diced vegetables and cook them for 2 to 3 minutes.

4) Add the vinegar, salt, pepper, and beef stock. Bring to a boil. Add the lentils, the spices tied in a cheesecloth, and the frankfurters.

5) Skim off the fat and add the Worcestershire sauce. Taste the soup. Adjust the seasoning, and let it cook until the lentils are soft.

☞ Roast Loin of Pork[3]

*Serves 8 to 12
(or fewer people, with
leftovers)*

16 dried prunes
1 four-pound boneless loin of pork
¼ cup oil
½ teaspoon salt
¼ teaspoon ground black pepper
2 cups brown *chaud-froid* (optional)[4]

1) Pit the prunes and place them in a mixing bowl. Add enough boiling water to cover them, and let them stand for 1 hour.

---

[3] In some respects this recipe is reminiscent of Charles Augustus Milverton. The dish, and Watson's description of Milverton's exterior, have much in common: They are both cold, plump, fatty. Holmes conjectured that Milverton's interior was of marble. For pork stuffing, however, an interior of prunes would be preferable. For the sake of Canonicity, one might begin with well-marbled meat.

[4] Mrs. Hudson probably glazed this roast with a brown *chaud-froid* to preserve it while it sat on the sideboard. A brown *chaud-froid* may be made by dissolving a package of unflavoured gelatine in brown sauce. The roast would be cooled, sliced, reshaped, and coated with the liquid cold *chaud-froid*. For more complete instructions concerning brown *chaud-froid*, see p. 116.

2) Make a pocket by running a sharp knife through the center of the pork loin. It may be necessary to insert the knife from both ends of the meat; trim away any excess fat.

3) Drain the prunes and insert them throughout the pocket of the pork. Tie the loin with string to retain its shape.

4) Place the meat in a roasting pan; pour the oil over it and season it with salt and pepper.

5) Bake it in a 400°F. oven for 1 hour and 45 minutes, or until the internal temperature is 185°. Turn the meat every ½ hour.

6) Cool the pork to room temperature and slice it ¼ to ½ inch thick. Arrange the piece of loin in the middle of the platter, and surround it with pork slices.

Serve the platter decorated with a bunch of watercress and stuffed green olives.

☞ Apple Sauce

See recipe, p. 29.

☞ English Dill Loaf

1 loaf

2⅓ cups flour
1½ ounces fresh compressed yeast
A pinch of sugar
¼ cup milk, at body temperature
2 onions
1 teaspoon dried dill
½ teaspoon salt
1¾ ounces melted butter or oil
2 eggs
½ teaspoon dill seeds

1) Put the flour into a large bowl. Press a cavity into the centre of the flour, and fill it with the yeast and sugar. Add the milk. Mix these ingredients together with a little of the adjacent flour to make a light dough that is of a watery consistency.

2) Put the dough aside in a warm place to rise until the dough in the centre has doubled in size.[5] This will take 20 to 25 minutes or longer.

3) Peel the onions and chop them very fine. Add them, together with the dill, salt, melted butter or oil, and eggs, into the centre of the dough.

4) Flour your hands and gradually mix in all of the flour, working in a spiral fashion out from the centre. Knead the dough well, until it is smooth and elastic and does not stick to the sides of the bowl.

5) Allow the dough to rise again for 20 to 30 minutes, or until it has doubled in size.

6) Shape it into a long loaf. Set it on a greased baking tray, and cut the top of the loaf slightly lengthwise. Brush it with water, and sprinkle it with dill seeds.

7) Allow it to rise for 15 to 20 minutes; then bake it in a preheated oven at 300°F. for 40 to 45 minutes. Brush the crust with water again after removing it from the oven.

☞ Gingerbread

    2 eggs, beaten
    ¾ cup brown sugar
    ¾ cup molasses
    ¾ cup melted shortening
    2¼ cups flour
    2 teaspoons ginger
    1½ teaspoons cinnamon
    2½ teaspoons baking powder
    ¾ teaspoon soda
    ½ teaspoon cloves
    ½ teaspoon nutmeg
    1 cup boiling water

1) Add the beaten eggs to the sugar, molasses, and shortening. Mix them together well.

2) Sift the flour together with all the other dry ingredients and add to the above mixture.

3) Pour in the hot water. Mix well, and pour the batter into 2 greased loaf pans or 1 greased shallow pan.

4) Bake in a moderate oven (350°F.) for 40 minutes.

---

[5] Do not let it rise more than double: "When one tries to rise above Nature, one is liable to fall below it." (Sherlock Holmes in "The Adventure of the Creeping Man.")

🖝 Epilogue

At the conclusion of this adventure Holmes and Watson came the closest they had ever come to sharing the same jail cell. Their clandestine visit to Milverton's premises did not go undiscovered, and they had to be fleet of foot indeed to elude their pursuers. The following morning after breakfast, our friends received a familiar visitor, Inspector Lestrade, who sought help "in a most remarkable case"—the events at the Milverton household the night before. One of the culprits was "a middle-sized, strongly built man—square jaw, thick neck, moustache . . ."

"That's rather vague," said Sherlock Holmes. "Why, it might be a description of Watson!"

"It's true," said the inspector, with amusement. "It might be a description of Watson."

The breakfast preceding this interlude is not difficult to deduce. Having provided cold roast pork the night before, Mrs. Hudson would, of course, have used the remainder in the breakfast.

🖝 Pork Fricassee

Serves 4

    1 pound leftovers, roasted or boiled pork, diced
    2 ounces butter
    1½ tablespoons flour
    2 cups chicken broth (may be made from bouillon cubes)
    1 egg yolk
    3 tablespoons white wine
    2 tablespoons heavy cream
    Juice of ½ lemon
    ⅓ teaspoon salt, or to taste

1) Melt the butter and add the flour. Stir together to make a roux. Add the chicken broth, and simmer for 15 minutes. Remove from the fire.

2) Mix the egg yolk, wine, heavy cream, and lemon juice. Fold them into the sauce. Taste and adjust the seasoning, starting with ⅓ teaspoon salt.

3) Add the diced pork, return the mixture to the fire, and bring it to one boil. Remove it from the heat as soon as it boils.

Serve it with toasted English muffins, toasted dill bread or patty shells.

Note: ½ teaspoon chopped parsley or 3 ounces canned mushrooms may be added with the pork.

An Epicurean Cold Supper

No meal in the entire Sherlockian Canon has provoked more discussion than the "epicurean cold supper" at the close of "The Adventure of the Noble Bachelor." The repast was enjoyed by Holmes, Watson, and two American guests, but was declined by Lord Robert St. Simon, for whom the story was named. This unfortunate nobleman did not have much to eat that day, it would seem, for he was unable to finish his wedding breakfast after his wealthy bride suddenly vanished. The state of Lord Robert's stomach does not fuel much debate, however, for to be, as Holmes put it, "deprived in an instant of wife and fortune" will most assuredly take the edge off a man's appetite.

The discussion, rather, is over the food served that evening. It is one of the few menus fully described in the Canon: "a couple of brace of cold woodcock, a pheasant, a *pâté de foie gras* pie, with a group of ancient and cobwebby bottles." The woodcock and pheasant have inspired some mouth-watering speculation,[1] but the *pâté de foie gras* pie, as we shall see, has engendered true controversy. First, the woodcock.

☞ Cold Woodcock

According to the Canon, the caterer supplied "a couple of brace of cold woodcock." A brace consists of two birds, a male and a female. We may presume, therefore, that four woodcock were among the viands laid out that night. Because the woodcock, in this instance, were prepared for cold service, to await the diners, unrefrigerated, for a matter of hours, we may assume that the usual practice of cooking it undrawn was defied as a precaution against food poisoning.[2] The precious entrails, considered by some

---

[1] For example, see Fletcher Pratt, "The Gastronomic Holmes," *Baker Street Journal,* 1952, 2 (new series), pp. 94–99.

[2] For further discussion on the cooking of woodcock, see p. 174.

gourmets to be the best part, were reserved, chopped, cooked separately and used to garnish the cold fowl.

To prepare the woodcock for the oven:

1) Pluck and eviscerate the bird; wash it thoroughly and dry it.

2) Remove the lower part of the beak, the esophagus, the crop, and the eyes; but leave the head and legs. Trim the claws.

To roast the woodcock:

Serves 4

    4 oven-ready woodcock
    2 teaspoons salt, or to taste
    16 peppercorns
    1 medium-sized onion, quartered (4 to 5 ounces)
    8 juniper berries
    8 stems of parsley
    4 bacon strips
    3 ounces butter, melted

1) Season each bird inside and outside with salt and pepper.

2) Stuff the cavity of each bird with 1 quarter onion, 2 juniper berries, and 2 parsley sprigs.

3) Truss the bird by folding the legs back into the cavity. Push the beak of the bird through the legs to act as a skewer.

4) Bard each woodcock by covering it with a strip of bacon. Brush them with melted butter and roast them in a 350° to 400°F. oven for 15 to 20 minutes, or until they are ready. Baste them as often as possible. Remove them and cool them before carving.

For an epicurean cold supper, the carving of the poultry is as important as its cooking. In the world of classical cuisine, the artistry of preparing food for cold service is called *garde manger* and is itself a culinary specialty.[3]

There are a number of ways to display cold woodcock. It was common practice, when a brace of woodcock were served, to carve the meatier female for immediate service, and to display the showier male with his plumage. The feathers, which had been removed, skin and all, were cured before being replaced.[4] The Englishman of Holmes's age was not as senti-

---

[3] We may safely presume that had Holmes became a chef, he would have been well skilled in *garde manger,* saying, as he did in *The Valley of Fear,* "Surely, our profession . . . would be a drab and sordid one if we did not sometimes set the scene so as to glorify our results."

[4] This effect may be produced today, of course, by using only one woodcock, and mounting the plumage on a styrofoam base. To quote Sherlock Holmes: "What you do . . . is a matter of no consequence. The question is, what you can make people believe that you have done." (*A Study in Scarlet.*)

mental about the animals he ate as is his counterpart today. A reminder of the creature in its living state did not suppress the appetite as it would for some modern diners. Furthermore, there was not the sanitarian's concern that the plumage might somehow contaminate the food. This was not, however, the only method of serving a brace of woodcock, and we will assume that it was not the display which was laid out on the mahogany of 221 B Baker Street.

To carve the roast woodcock:

1) Cut off the neck and head.

2) With the neck end of the woodcock facing you, gently cut through the meat on either side of the breastbone, stopping when the knife meets resistance. By placing your thumbs under the meat at the neck end, gently lift the breast of the woodcock off the carcass. The meat on either side should come off in one piece.

3) Sharply twist the breastbone and wishbone out of the breast fillets.

4) Fill the breast cavity with liver mousse (see recipe for *Pâté de Foie Gras Pie,* page 116).

5) Cut each breast fillet in half lengthwise and place it on top of the liver mousse.

6) Use the beak of the woodcock as a decorative skewer.

☞ Cold Roast Pheasant

Serves 2 to 4

    1 oven-ready pheasant
    ½ to 1 teaspoon salt, or to taste
    3 grinds of black pepper, or to taste
    1 rib celery
    1 carrot
    1 quarter of a medium-sized onion (4 to 5 ounces)
    1 bay leaf
    2 sprigs parsley
    4 juniper berries
    2 ounces butter, melted
    1 slice of bacon

1) Rinse the pheasant well and dry it. Season it inside and outside with salt and pepper.

2) Fill the cavity with the celery, carrot, onion, bay leaf, parsley, and juniper berries.

3) Brush the pheasant with the melted butter. Bard it by placing the bacon slice on top of it.

4) Roast it in a 350°F. oven for ½ to ¾ hour. Allow it to cool. Remove the vegetables from the interior and carve it according to the instructions which follow.

Note: The vegetables may be diced and mixed with about 1 to 2 tablespoons of mayonnaise to make a salad, and served with the pheasant.

In order to carve the pheasant properly, it will be useful to have very sharp knives at your disposal, preferably a French knife (one with a broad 10-inch blade), and a paring or boning knife.

1) Begin carving by making a cut in the skin where the leg and the breast connect.

2) Place the pheasant on its side. Beginning immediately beneath the wing, cut the meat in a circular pattern along the backbone, following the bone structure. Cut until you reach the joint of the leg. Cut gently through the leg joint. Repeat the process with the other side of the pheasant.

3) With the front (neck) of the pheasant facing you, make one cut on either side of the breastbone, cutting gently until you can go no further. Place both thumbs in the neck cavity and pull the meat loose from the carcass. Each breast fillet should come off in one piece.

4) With a sharp twist, lift the wishbone and the breastbone out of the breast fillets. (At this point the pheasant is in 4 pieces.)

5) Remove the wings from the breast pieces by cutting them at the joint.

6) If the blade bone has adhered to the leg meat, remove it. Remove the tiny fillets (the "oysters") which rest on the blade, and save them. (Or eat them on the spot. They're the best part of the bird!)

7) Cut the pheasant through each leg joint, making 4 pieces.

8) To carve the breast fillets, start 2 inches behind the point where the wing connects and cut through it at a 45° angle. Make another cut about 2 inches behind that, thereby cutting each breast portion into 3 pieces.

9) To arrange the pheasant on the platter, arrange the leg pieces and breast pieces as they would lie had the bird been split in half lengthwise. Put the two wing bones together as if in flight. Place these at either the top or the bottom of the arrangement.

10) Garnish the platter with watercress, dill, or parsley.

This manner of carving will give an epicurean touch to even the most plebeian barbecued chickens sold in the supermarket.

Before garnishing the roast woodcock and pheasant, Holmes's caterer coated both displays with brown *chaud-froid*. By coating the entire surface of the meat with this sauce, they prolonged the time during which the food could be kept unrefrigerated before it spoiled. This sauce is named *chaud-froid* from the French because it is prepared warm (*chaud*) and used cold (*froid*).[5] With modern refrigeration, *chaud-froid* is rarely necessary today except as a decoration, to provide a classical look. To prepare and apply a brown *chaud-froid,* follow these steps:

1) Place the item to be coated on a wire rack with a sheet pan underneath it to catch the drippings.

2) Prepare a brown *chaud-froid* by dissolving a package of unflavoured gelatine in 1 pint of Brown Sauce (see recipe, p. 159).

3) Cool the sauce over ice, stirring continuously, until it will coat your fingernail without dripping off.

4) Apply the brown *chaud-froid* in a thin, even layer to the bird, beginning first with the sides and then the top. Chill it on ice, or, yes, by using a refrigerator. If it is not completely covered, apply two or three more coats, having chilled the meat between coats. The coating should be as smooth as possible. The sauce is kept smooth during the application by reheating it slightly in the top of a double boiler whenever lumps appear. The sauce which has collected in the sheet pan may be reheated and used. If the result is too lumpy, the sauce may be scraped off and reapplied.

Pâté de Foie Gras *Pie à la Watson*

The little problem of the *pâté de foie gras* pie was brought to the attention of the Sherlockian world by noted mystery writer Marie Rodell,[6] who "hunted through the works of the culinary experts of Victoria's reign," and found no such thing as *pâté de foie gras* pie. After weighing the various explanations which fit this undeniable fact, she concluded that possibly "it was Watson himself who invented *pâté de foie gras* pie."

Whereupon Baker Street Irregular Morris Rosenblum immediately jumped to the defense of Watson.[7] Through his researches he found, not

---

[5] For a complete treatise on all types of *chaud-froid*, we recommend Frederic Sonnenschmidt and Jean Nicolas, *The Professional Chef's Art of Garde Manger*, Boston: Cahners, 1973.

[6] "Living on Baker Street," *Baker Street Journal*, 1947, 2 (old series), pp. 84–89.

[7] In a letter to the editor of the *Baker Street Journal*, 1947, 2 (old series), pp. 438–439.

"*pâté de foie gras* pie," but "Strasbourg pie." By showing that Strasbourg pie was a pie of *pâté de foie gras*, he proved to his own satisfaction that Watson referred to a bona fide dish.

Much as we would like to vouch for Watson's accuracy in this matter, the painful truth is that in culinary terms, one does not speak of *pâté de foie gras* "pie." In a recent reopening of the great *pâté* debate, Patsy Dalton, of the Sherlock Holmes Society of London, explained why.[8] As originally defined by the French, a *pâté* is a filling of meat, fish, vegetables, or fruit in a pastry case, *i.e.*, a pie. In recent usage, the term *pâté* has come to refer only to the meat or fish preparations themselves.[9] We may infer that Watson, knowing that this distinction had been blurred, had chosen to make the form of the *pâté* explicit by adding the word "pie." In the culinary world, this distinction is correctly made by adding the words "*en croute*" to designate the liver concoction when it is enclosed in pastry.

We may defend Watson's accuracy, therefore, to the extent that he saw the need to clarify the ambiguity of the word "*pâté*," but did not do it in the traditional way. We found some evidence to justify this mistake in two American cookbooks of the Holmesian era. Both of them list *pâté de foie gras* in the chapter on pies. It is natural to combine the title of the dish with the chapter heading to come up with the name "*pâté de foie gras* pie." This argument presumes that Watson was familiar with American cookbooks, and leads inescapably to the conclusion that Watson had lived for some time in the United States.[10] Doubtless he shared the sentiments expressed by Holmes as they and their American guests prepared to enjoy the epicurean cold supper: "It is always a joy to meet an American . . . for I am one of those who believe that the folly of a monarch and the blundering of a minister in far-gone years will not prevent our children from being some day citizens of the same world-wide country under a flag which shall be a quartering of the Union Jack with the Stars and Stripes."

We considered, for a moment, offering one of the old American recipes as the *pâté de foie gras* pie for this epicurean meal. Examination of the recipes themselves showed that neither of them was suitable. The first recipe, although it was attributed to a Mr. Delmonico, was virtually incompre-

[8] "Canon Fodder," *Sherlock Holmes Journal*, 1974, *11*, pp. 112–116.

[9] To further confuse matters in the culinary world, the term "*pâté*" is also used to describe any preparation put into an earthenware dish that has been lined with thin layers of fresh pork fat and is then baked in the oven. The correct name for this dish, however, is "terrine."

[10] According to Holmes's biographer, William S. Baring-Gould, Dr. Watson was in the United States from 1884 to 1886. While he was there, according to Baring-Gould, practicing medicine in San Francisco, he met his first wife, Miss Constance Adams, who died after little more than one year of marriage. (*Sherlock Holmes of Baker Street*, New York: Clarkson N. Potter, 1962.)

hensible.[11] If it were to be followed as written, it would produce an incredibly greasy liver mixture enclosed in the residue of a squashed, over-cooked puff paste. We hope that if the Mr. Delmonico who contributed the recipe was the Delmonico of the famous restaurant, his chef knew better. The second recipe was more nearly usable, but it suffered from an opposite defect.[12] It would have been too dry for lack of sufficient fat.

It is not possible to deduce the precise formula by which the Canonical *pâté de foie gras* pie was made. It could have been a *pâté* which, strictly speaking, begins with uncooked ground meat which is cooked with the pastry, or it could have been a pie of *foie gras* which began with cooked ground meat—for example, a liver mousse—and was served in a baked pie shell. All things considered, including taste, craftsmanship, and what Watson probably saw, we have selected the latter.

☞ Pâté de Foie Gras Pie[13]

Makes one 9-inch pie

1 pound goose or chicken livers
Buttermilk or milk
Sherry wine
1/2 pound pork fat, chopped
2 tablespoons shallots, finely chopped
1/2 cup mushroom trimmings, chopped
1 teaspoon salt, or to taste
1/8 teaspoon pepper, or to taste
1/3 teaspoon *Pâté* Spice (see recipe, p. 119)
1/3 teaspoon thyme
1 small bay leaf

[11] Elizabeth Fries Ellet. *The Practical Housekeeper: A Cyclopaedia of Domestic Economy*, New York: Stringer and Townsend, 1857, pp. 412–413. Reproduced in Albert M. Rosenblatt, "On *Pâté de Foie Gras* Pie: In Defense of Watson," *Baker Street Journal*, 1973, 23, p. 103.

[12] Sarah Tyson Rorer. *Mrs. Rorer's Philadelphia Cookbook*, Philadelphia: Arnold, 1886, p. 487.

[13] This is a recipe to challenge the whole art of detection, for it may be made without the slightest bit of *foie gras*, the liver of the specially fattened geese of Strasbourg. At the time of this writing, genuine fresh *foie gras* markets for approximately $125 per pound, a price which may exceed the budgets of some readers. For similar reasons, one might wish to omit the truffles, which currently sell for over $110 per pound. There are mock truffles on the market, based upon charcoal powder and gelatine, which may be used if desired. This pie was served at the Culinary Institute of America dinner of June 2, 1973.

2 to 4 tablespoons unflavoured gelatine (2 to 4 packages)
2 cups meat stock
2 tablespoons Madeira wine
2 tablespoons brandy
½ cup heavy cream
Diced black and white truffles (optional)
1 baked pie shell

1) Marinate the livers for 24 hours in buttermilk or milk. Then rinse them thoroughly and dry them. Marinate them for 24 hours more in sherry wine.

2) Melt the pork fat in a pan, and sauté the chicken livers. Do not over-cook the livers; leave them pink.

3) Remove the livers from the pan, and cook the shallots and mush-rooms in the pork fat. Add the seasonings and herbs.

4) Mix these ingredients well. Cool them, combine with the livers, and puree all in a blender.

5) Combine the gelatine and stock in a small saucepan. Stir it gently over low heat until the gelatine dissolves. Remove it from the heat and add the 2 tablespoons of Madeira. (Test the strength of the gelatine by putting 1 teaspoon of it in the refrigerator. If it does not jell, add more gelatine.)

6) Mix the liver preparation, brandy, heavy cream and 6 to 8 ounces of the gelatine solution in a blender. Remove from blender and fold in the truffles (if used). Test the mixture for jelling as in Step 5. If it does not set, add more of the gelatine mixture. Pour it into the baked pie shell and chill it.

7) Pour the remainder of the Madeira aspic into a pan in a layer about ¼ inch thick. Cut it into appropriate shapes for decoration.

☞ Pâté Spice (Épice Marie)

6 bay leaves
1 tablespoon thyme
1 tablespoon whole coriander seed
1 tablespoon cinnamon
½ tablespoon cloves
1 tablespoon nutmeg
1 tablespoon ginger
1 tablespoon mace
1 tablespoon black peppercorns (or ½ tablespoon ground black
    pepper)

1 tablespoon white peppercorns (or ½ tablespoon ground white
  pepper)
¼ teaspoon cayenne

Mix all the spices thoroughly in a blender. This is the minimum amount
that can be effectively mixed in the blender. The mixture will keep virtually indefinitely if stored in a tightly covered jar.

Dinner for Two:
A Pleasant Reunion

In "The Adventure of the Mazarin Stone," we come to the twilight of
Sherlock Holmes's career as a consulting detective, the dramatic repposses-
sion of a stolen diamond, and a quiet dinner of reunion between the Detective and his Boswell.

Dr. Watson had abandoned Baker Street for matrimony the second (or
was it the third or the fourth?) time, but he occasionally returned to Baker
Street for old-times' sake. Dr. Watson's marriages have engendered much
debate among Sherlockian critics. His marriage to Mary Morstan shortly
after *The Sign of Four* in 1887 or 1888 is incontrovertible. A bereavement
during 1891–1894 is well established on Canonical authority. A marriage
late in 1902, the one referred to in "The Mazarin Stone," also cannot be
denied. Several critics, confounding deductive powers with imagination,
have invented additional marriages for the retired Army doctor. New marriages account for the curious absence of adventures in certain years, and
one fabrication explains the adventures that encounter a married Watson,
but might otherwise have occurred before he met Mary Morstan. So
many brief journeys into wedlock have been proposed for Watson that
the late Dorothy Sayers was led to exclaim, "Watson should seem to have
been rather a perilous marriage partner, and . . . it might have been advisable to check up the contents of his poison cupboard."[1] At the other

---

[1] "Dr. Watson, Widower," in *Unpopular Opinions,* London: Victor Gollancz, Ltd.,
1946, p. 167, n. 1.

extreme, however, there remains the possibility that Watson was married only once, and the bereavement in 1891–1894 was the loss of another family member, perhaps a child. If so, the alternating periods of absence and residence at Baker Street were the result of periodic marital strife, occasioned by continual conflict between Sherlock Holmes and Mary Morstan Watson. In considering this possibility, we should have to note that Mary won in the end, for Sherlock Holmes retired to Sussex alone. Whatever marriage it was in number,[2] the 1902 matrimony was Dr. Watson's final departure from Baker Street. Thereafter, when he came to see Holmes, it was only to visit. At the time of the Mazarin Stone, "It was pleasant to Dr. Watson to find himself once more in the untidy room of the first floor on Baker Street which had been the starting point of so many remarkable adventures."

Watson chose a most fortuitous time to call on his friend. He was on hand for the dramatic culmination of Holmes's investigation into a hundred-thousand-pound burglary, in which a large yellow diamond—the Mazarin Stone[3]—had been stolen. Holmes had discovered the thieves. It remained to recover the stone. While Watson went for Scotland Yard, Holmes engaged in one of his dramatic deceptions in which he tricked the thieves into revealing the diamond.

When all was finished, a quiet, joyful meal was in order: ". . . tell Mrs. Hudson that I should be glad if she would send up dinner for two as soon as possible."

> Tomato Cocktail
> Fillet of Haddock Mazarin
> Boiled Leeks
> Duchess Potatoes
> Bread Pudding
> Fresh Fruit[4]

Although it is not usually within our province to suggest dinner music, we should note that to have the "Barcarolle" from Offenbach's *The Tales*

---

[2] On the subject of Dr. Watson's proposed marriages, Ronald DeWaal lists 29 separate articles (*The World Bibliography of Sherlock Holmes and Dr. Watson*, Boston: The New York Graphic Society, 1974). Undoubtedly his planned supplement will include many more on this inexhaustible subject.

[3] The diamond was evidently named for Cardinal Jules Mazarin (1602–1661), a famous diamond collector. Eminent Sherlockian Peter Blau has noted, however, that none of the diamonds from Mazarin's collection matches the one described in this adventure. He has identified the stone as one of the Crown Diamonds of Persia, owned at that time by Muzaffer ad-Din. By discreetly restoring the jewel to its owner, Holmes once more prevented an embarrassing international incident. (Peter Blau, "In Memoriam: Muzaffer ad-Din," *Baker Street Journal*, 1974, *24*, pp. 141–145.)

[4] Holmes and Watson, we fancy, finished their meal with imported fresh fruit from a basket bearing the name "Castalotte and Zamba, New York City," which had been delivered with a note of thanks for Holmes's help in the matter of the Red Circle.

of *Hoffmann* playing quietly in the background would lend authenticity. Holmes, it will be noted, did so in "The Adventure of the Mazarin Stone."

☞ **Tomato Cocktail**

Serves 4

> 4 large tomatoes
> Juice of 1 lemon
> 4 tablespoons oil
> ½ teaspoon salt
> ½ teaspoon crushed black pepper
> 4 tablespoons tomato catsup[5]
> Frozen Creamed Horseradish (see recipe below)
> 2 teaspoons caviar (optional)

1) Blanch[6] the tomatoes, peel them, and dice them after removing the seeds.

2) Marinate the tomatoes in the lemon juice, oil, salt, and pepper for 10 minutes.

3) Put the marinated tomatoes into 4 champagne glasses and top each with a spoonful of tomato catsup, a little frozen creamed horseradish, and, if desired, a little caviar.

FROZEN CREAMED HORSERADISH

Makes 1½ cups

> ½ cup heavy cream
> 1 to 2 tablespoons prepared or frozen horseradish
> 1 teaspoon distilled white vinegar
> ⅓ teaspoon salt, or to taste
> ⅓ teaspoon black pepper, coarsely crushed

---

[5] We tend to think of tomato catsup as an abomination of our modern age, but it was popular in Victorian days. It was homemade, of course, and was usually lacking that burnt, somewhat metallic taste that we today have come to know and love.

[6] This procedure recalls "The Adventure of the Blanched Soldier" in which Holmes's intervention led to correcting the tragic misdiagnosis of Godfrey Emsworth's affliction.

1) Whip the heavy cream. Combine it with the horseradish, vinegar, salt, and pepper.

2) Spread a sheet of waxed paper lightly with oil.

3) Roll the horseradish mixture in the waxed paper, making a cylinder that is about 1½ inches in diameter, and freeze it.

4) At serving time, unroll the waxed paper and cut the frozen cylinder into slices. Use it to garnish the tomato cocktail, or other dishes such as salmon, trout, smoked ham, or veal and ham pie.

Note: This recipe makes much more sauce than will be needed to garnish the 4 tomato cocktails given above. It is, however, difficult to make in smaller quantities. The sauce will keep well in the freezer. The slices may be cut while the sauce cylinder is frozen, and the remainder returned to the freezer before it has been allowed to thaw.

☞ Fillet of Haddock Mazarin[7]

Serves 4

4 haddock fillets (6 ounces each)
4 shallots, finely chopped (2 ounces)
1½ ounces butter
½ to 1 teaspoon salt
⅓ teaspoon white pepper, or to taste
½ pound fresh mushrooms, sliced
1 cup white wine
1 tablespoon chopped parsley
1 tablespoon butter
1 tablespoon flour
1 cup fish stock or water
2 egg yolks
⅓ cup heavy cream, whipped
⅓ cup crabmeat, diced
4 medium or jumbo shrimp, cooked and peeled
4 truffles or 4 slices of black olive

[7] We were tempted to call for shark and gudgeon in this dish, for the villain of this piece, Count Negretto Sylvius, and his companion, Sam Merton, the boxer, were thus referred to by Holmes. Shark would be suitable, but not as good as haddock. Gudgeon, however, would not be a good substitution. It is a small, minnow-like fish, used, if at all, only for a garnish. This recipe is our adaptation of a dish named for Cardinal Mazarin and listed by Chef Dietman Barnikell in *A Biographical Sketch of Who Is Who on the Menu,* which was published serially in *The Culinarian,* the official publication of the Chefs' Association of the Pacific Coast.

1) Spread the shallots out in a well-buttered shallow casserole. Place the fish, side by side, on top of the shallots. Season them with salt and pepper.

2) Add the mushrooms, ¾ cup of white wine, and the parsley.

3) Cover with a piece of buttered paper or waxed paper with a hole in the center. Bring to a boil on top of the stove, then place in a 350°F. oven until the fish is done (5 to 10 minutes).

4) Remove the fish to a serving tray and keep it warm.

5) Reduce the liquid in the casserole to a syrup consistency.

6) Melt the 1 tablespoon of butter in a saucepan, stir in the flour and mix it thoroughly. Add the fish stock or water, and stir until the sauce begins to thicken. Add the sauce to the reduced casserole liquid.

7) Bring it to one boil and remove it from the fire.

8) Add the egg yolks. Fold in the whipped cream and add the crabmeat.

9) Heat the shrimp in the remaining white wine.

10) Pour the sauce over the fish and glaze it under a broiler. Top each fillet with a shrimp and a truffle or a slice of black olive.

☞ Boiled Leeks

Serves 4

> 8 large leeks
> Chopped fresh parsley
> Melted butter

1) Use only the white part of the leeks. Wash them very well to remove the sand. Tie them together with a string.

2) Cook them in enough salted water to cover for about 20 to 25 minutes or until they are tender.

3) Drain them and serve them on a folded napkin or perforated asparagus dish. Garnish them with chopped fresh parsley, and serve them with melted butter.

☞ Duchess Potatoes

Serves 4

> 1 pound potatoes
> 2 ounces butter

2 egg yolks or 1 whole egg
½ to 1 teaspoon salt, or to taste
⅓ teaspoon white pepper
A pinch of nutmeg
1 egg mixed with 1 tablespoon milk

1) Peel the potatoes and cut them into quarters. Boil them in salted water.

2) When they are done, drain them, and put them in a warm oven for a few minutes to evaporate the excess moisture.

3) Mash them through a sieve. Mix in the butter, the 2 egg yolks, and seasonings.

4) Put them into a well-greased fireproof dish. Brush the top with the egg-and-milk mixture and bake them at 350° to 400°F. until they are brown.

☞ Bread Pudding

Serves 4

6 slices white bread
1 cup milk
2¾ ounces margarine or butter
3 eggs, separated
1 tablespoon sugar
3 to 4 heaping tablespoons raisins
Grated peel of half a lemon
1 to 2 ounces grated almonds
Butter or margarine to grease the mould

1) Remove the crusts from the slices of white bread.

2) Soak the bread in the milk.

3) Melt the margarine or butter and heat the soaked bread in it.

4) Remove it from the fire and cool it. Fold the egg yolks slowly into the bread mixture.

5) Mix in the sugar, raisins, lemon peel, and grated almonds.

6) Whip the egg whites until they are stiff, and fold them into the mixture.

7) Grease a fireproof 1-quart casserole or Pyrex mixing bowl and fill it with the bread mixture.

8) Bake it uncovered in a preheated 350° to 375°F. oven for 30 minutes. It may be served hot or cold.

Retirement in Sussex

Curiously, because Mr. Sherlock Holmes could not abide idleness,[1] in 1903 he expressed the wish to retire.[2] Soon thereafter, he had withdrawn to his "little Sussex home." The full explanation for his retirement will remain a mystery. Advancing years will not fully account for it. Taking the usually accepted year of birth, 1854, he was only about 50 years old when he gave himself "up entirely to that soothing life of Nature for which [he] had so often yearned during the long years spent amid the gloom of London."[3]

Early in 1902, Watson wrote that "Holmes had spent several days in bed, as was his habit from time to time."[4] Taken alone, this might not be worthy of notice. For as long as Watson had known him, the Master was subject to periods of depression. But by September of that year Watson had moved to his "own rooms in Queen Anne Street."[5] Before the new year, Watson had married. Surely the courtship and marriage was a blow to Holmes, who early on had said, "I am lost without my Boswell."[6]

Holmes must have missed Watson. In 1903, Watson admitted that "The relations between us in those latter days were peculiar." Occasionally Watson received an urgent summons: "Come at once if convenient—if

---

[1] "My mind rebels at stagnation. Give me problems, give me work, give me the most abstruse cryptogram, or the most intricate analysis, and I am in my own proper atmosphere. . . . I abhor the dull routine of existence. I crave for mental exaltation." (*The Sign of Four.*)

[2] "It's surely time that I disappeared into that little farm of my dreams." ("The Adventure of the Creeping Man.")

[3] "The Adventure of the Lion's Mane." This statement is all the more startling when it is compared with Watson's statement that "appreciation of Nature found no place among his many gifts" (from "The Adventure of the Cardboard Box"/"Resident Patient"), but Watson was not always correct in assessing the Master's proclivities.

[4] He was aroused from his lethargy by the problem presented in "The Adventure of the Three Garridebs."

[5] In "The Adventure of the Illustrious Client."

[6] In "A Scandal in Bohemia," which took place during Watson's first marriage.

inconvenient come all the same.—S.H."[7] It was difficult for the Great Detective to work without Watson as a sounding board for his ideas. The good doctor was more than just a chronicler. He was an essential part of the work, a whetstone for the mind.

The way of life in Sussex was much different from that in London. Holmes wrote in 1907, "My house is lonely. I, my old housekeeper, and my bees have the estate all to ourselves."[8] For "mental excitation"—except for an occasional mystery like that self-recorded in "The Adventure of the Lion's Mane"—Holmes had only his bees. He worked at beekeeping in much the same manner that he did at sleuthing. Within a few years, he had written the *Practical Handbook of Bee Culture, with Some Observations Upon the Segregation of the Queen:* "Behold the fruit of pensive nights and laborious days when I watched the little working gangs as once I watched the criminal world of London."[9] The young retiree was not entirely idle.

What about his loneliness? We assert that he married. His objection to matrimony was that emotion would interfere with his reasoning ability. Having renounced detection, he had no reason not to take a wife. Holmes has even left a clue to the identity of his bride. In "The Adventure of the Lion's Mane" he wrote of the lovely Maude Bellamy: "There was no gainsaying that she would have graced any assembly in the world. Who would have guessed that so rare a flower would grow from such a root and in such an atmosphere. Women have seldom been an attraction to me, for my brain has always governed my heart, but I could not look on her perfect clear-cut face, with all the soft freshness of the downlands in her delicate colouring, without realizing that no young man would cross her path unscathed." Not only a young man, but the mature Sherlock Holmes was susceptible to her charms.

We can visualize the lonely little house, not so lonely any more. Sherlock Holmes, his lovely wife Maude, and their elderly housekeeper were there. Many critics believe that Mrs. Hudson followed the Master into retirement, remaining as his housekeeper in Sussex. If so, her cooking served as one reminder of those active days at 221B Baker Street.

A RETIREMENT MENU

Violets in Beer Batter
Thick Oxtail Soup

[7] This was the summons to "The Adventure of the Creeping Man."
[8] "The Adventure of the Lion's Mane."
[9] "His Last Bow."

Honey-Cured Duck
Rice Pilaf with Raisins and Nuts
Martha's Melon Pickle
Apple Fritters

☞ Violets in Beer Batter[10]

Wash the violet flowers well and drain them. Dip the individual flowers into beer batter and deep-fry them to a golden crisp.

BEER BATTER

Makes 1½ pints

2 cups flour
½ can or 7-ounce bottle of beer
1 egg yolk
A pinch of salt
2 egg whites, whipped

Mix the flour, beer, egg yolk, and salt until the mixture becomes a liquid paste. Whip the egg whites to a stiff meringue and fold them into the liquid paste. Allow the batter to rest for 1 hour before using it. This batter keeps well in the refrigerator and improves with age, up to about 5 days.

☞ Thick Oxtail Soup

Serves 4

2 to 3 pounds oxtail, cut into 1½ to 2-inch pieces
½ cup shortening

---

[10] These edible spring flowers reminded Sherlock Holmes of the many young women named Violet whom he befriended. Violet Smith, who cycled her way into peril; Violet Hunter, who found danger and adventure at the "Copper Beeches"; Violet de Merville, saved from a fate worse than death through the intervention of an "Illustrious Client"; and Violet Westbury, whose fiancé had come to grief in "The Adventure of the Bruce-Partington Plans."

1 medium-sized onion, sliced
4 large carrots, diced
2 tablespoons flour
2 parsnips, diced
2 celery ribs, diced
2 quarts water
1 teaspoon coarse (Kosher) salt
1 cup Madeira wine
A pinch each of marjoram, sage, rosemary, and thyme[11]

1) Blanch the pieces of oxtail for 2 minutes in boiling water, then rinse them with cold water.

2) Melt the shortening in a deep pot. Brown the oxtail, the onion, and 2 of the carrots.

3) Sprinkle with the flour, and stir well. Cook the mixture until it takes on a rich brown color. (This cooking may be accomplished in the oven at 350° to 400°F.)

4) Cook the remaining carrots, the parsnips, and the celery in 2 quarts of salted water until they are tender. Drain them and set aside to cool, reserving the water for the soup.

5) Add the reserved vegetable water to the meat. Cover and simmer slowly for 3 hours. (This should be done in the oven at 350° to 400°F.)

6) Strain the soup while it is hot; set aside the meat pieces.

7) Heat the Madeira wine to a boil, and mix it with the herbs. Allow it to rest for 20 minutes, then strain it into the soup. Taste it and adjust the seasoning.

8) Dice the oxtail meat and add it and the reserved vegetables to the soup. Serve very hot.

☞ Honey-Cured Duck

Serves 4

A 3- to 3½-pound duck
2 cups coarse salt
⅓ teaspoon thyme
⅓ teaspoon sage
⅓ teaspoon allspice
⅓ teaspoon ginger

---

[11] Gathered from the thyme-scented hills of Sussex.

1 cup brown sugar
¾ cup honey
½ cup dry white wine

1) Rinse the duck. Dry it well with a cloth.

2) Mix together the salt, spices, and sugar. Rub the duck with the salt mixture, and pack the rest of the mixture around the duck.

3) Cure it for 24 hours in the refrigerator, turning it 4 or 5 times.

4) At the end of this period, remove the duck and rinse it inside and outside. Drain and dry it.

5) Brush the duck with the honey. Marinate it for 24 hours in the honey, turning it 4 or 5 times.

6) At the end of this second 24-hour period, put ⅓ to ½ cup of water into a roasting pan. Add the duck with the honey and roast it in a preheated 325° to 350°F. oven for 45 to 50 minutes. Baste it with the honey mixture while it is roasting.

7) Remove the duck, drain off the fat, and deglaze the pan with the ½ cup of dry white wine. Strain the liquid and use it as a sauce.

☞ Rice Pilaf with Raisins and Nuts

Serves 4

2 tablespoons finely chopped onion
2 tablespoons butter
1 cup uncooked rice
4 tablespoons raisins
4 tablespoons nuts
2 cups water
1 teaspoon salt
1 carrot, peeled and cut in half
1 celery rib

1) Sauté the chopped onion in the butter.

2) Add the rice to it, and sauté it for 1 minute.

3) Add the raisins and nuts. Mix them well. Stir in the water and salt. Top the rice with the carrot halves and the celery stick.

4) Bring to a boil, cover, and finish in a preheated 400°F. oven for 20 minutes.

5) Remove from the oven; remove the carrot and celery and save them to eat later. Stir well and serve immediately.

☞ **Martha's Melon Pickle**[12]

Serves 4 to 6

1 ripe, firm cantaloupe (1 pound)
½ teaspoon alum[13]
2¾ cups water
1 cup sugar
⅔ cup vinegar
1 piece stick cinnamon
⅓ tablespoon allspice
½ teaspoon whole cloves

1) Pare and seed the cantaloupe. Cut it into 1-inch cubes.

2) Dissolve the alum in 2¼ cups water in a heavy kettle.

3) Heat to a boil. Add the cantaloupe and cook it for 10 minutes.

4) Drain the cantaloupe and rinse it well.

5) Combine the sugar, vinegar, ½ cup water, and spices tied in a piece of cheesecloth. Heat to boiling. Add the melon and cook slowly, covered, until the fruit is transparent, about 45 minutes.

6) Remove the spice bag. Pour the pickle mixture into a glass jar and refrigerate it.

☞ **Apple Fritters**

Serves 4 to 6

1 pound apples (3 to 4 medium-sized apples)
½ cup sugar
2 tablespoons rum
Beer Batter (Use the batter left over from the violets, see page 128.)

[12] Traditionally, oranges are served with duck, but often Mrs. Hudson substituted something else. Oranges always renewed for Holmes the painful memory of John Openshaw, whose life was lost in "The Adventure of the Five Orange Pips" in spite of Holmes's efforts on his behalf. Mrs. Hudson's first name is presumed to be Martha because that is how Holmes addressed his housekeeper in "His Last Bow."

[13] Not to be confused with anything having to do with "The Singular Affair of the Aluminum Crutch," referred to all too briefly in "The Musgrave Ritual," this substance may be readily purchased at a pharmacy. Alum may at some time have been a subject of one of Sherlock Holmes's investigations, for it was known to have been used in dangerously large quantities as a whitener for bread. It is used safely in this recipe to keep the pickles crisp.

Fat for frying

$\frac{1}{2}$ teaspoon cinnamon

1) Peel the apples and cut them into fairly thick slices. Cut out the cores.

2) Dredge them with sugar. Sprinkle them with rum, and let them rest for 1 hour.

3) Wipe them, dip them in the batter, and fry them in deep fat.

4) Drain them and dust them with the cinnamon mixed with sugar.

☞

On the Chase

The Start of a Brilliant Career

A disturbing thought it may be, but had Sherlock Holmes not accepted a certain invitation from his school friend, Victor Trevor,[1] he might have lived out his days as an obscure chemist or (can we suppose?) an unsuccessful ophthalmologist. It was while he was vacationing at Trevor's home that Holmes realized for the first time "that a profession might be made out of what had up to that time been the merest hobby."

The catalyst to Holmes's career, Victor Trevor, was introduced to Watson's public in the adventure known as "The *Gloria Scott*." Trevor himself was introduced to Holmes by Trevor's bull pup, who sank his teeth into

---

[1] Holmes referred to Trevor as "the only friend I made during the two years I was at college." We will not presume to enter the debate over the identity of Holmes's university, but rather we refer the reader to Ronald B. DeWaal, *The World Bibliography of Sherlock Holmes and Dr. Watson*, Boston: New York Graphic Society, 1974, pp. 179–181.

Holmes's ankle one morning on the way to chapel. The bite must have been severe, because its victim was laid up for ten days. The dog's owner visited Holmes regularly during the convalescence, and before long the two were good friends. When the school term ended, Holmes was invited to the Trevor estate at Donnithorpe in Norfolk.

Fortunately for the world, Sherlock Holmes found the "excellent wild-duck shooting in the fens, remarkably good fishing, a small but select library . . . and a tolerable cook," to say nothing of friendship, an adequate inducement to "put in a pleasant month there." Over a glass of port after dinner, the course of his life was changed. In pleasant relaxation and with more brilliance than tact, young Holmes deduced some distressing facts about his friend's father's past. Blanched with fear, the elder Trevor asked his guest the source of his information. Upon learning how young Sherlock had deduced so much from so little, he suggested that detection become the young student's future profession.

The dinner, we fancy, profited from the excellent hunting and fishing available to the Trevors and their guest—freshly caught pike and a dainty dish of young wild duck:

Iced Beef Broth
Pike—Farmer Style
Parsley Potatoes
White Wine Sherbet
Wild Duck the Hunter's Way
Sugared Orange Slices
Buttered String Beans
Strawberry Torte
Walnuts
Port

☞ Iced Beef Broth

Serves 4 to 6

½ pound beef shank or lean beef
¼ pound beef bones
8 cups water
1 teaspoon unflavoured gelatine
1 teaspoon salt, or to taste
1 whole leek (4 ounces)
1 rib celery (2 ounces)

1 carrot (2½ ounces)
1 small onion (1½ ounces)
1 clove garlic
2 tomatoes (6 ounces)
½ pound lean beef, coarsely ground
A pinch of nutmeg
½ bunch chives (10 chives)

1) Rinse the meat and the bones well. Place them in a large pot. Add 8 cups of cold water and the teaspoon of gelatine, and bring to a boil. Skim. Add the salt.

2) Clean and dice the leek, celery, carrot, and onion.

3) Sauté them in a pan without fat.

4) Peel the garlic and cut it into 4 pieces.

5) Rinse the tomatoes and cut them into wedges.

6) Put all the vegetables into the broth and simmer them for approximately 3 hours.

7) Remove all the fat from the broth. Strain the broth and pour it over the ground beef. Simmer it over a low fire for 15 to 20 minutes.

8) Strain the broth again. Season it with nutmeg and salt.

9) Cool it; remove all fat, and cool it further for 60 minutes in the refrigerator.

10) Chop the chives and sprinkle them over the soup. Serve it ice cold.

☞ Pike—Farmer Style[2]

Serves 4 to 6

1 three-pound pike
5 small onions (8 ounces)
6 ounces butter
1 to 2 teaspoons salt, or to taste
6 grinds of pepper, or to taste
1 ounce anchovy paste
Peel of half a lemon

---

[2] It was while fishing for this pike that Holmes made one of the discoveries that embarrassed his host: "When you bared your arm to draw that fish into the boat, I saw that J. A. had been tattooed in the bend on the elbow . . ." Pike was to reappear throughout the Detective's career: the pike to be found in Shoscombe Pond ("The Adventure of Shoscombe Old Place"); the villain Stapleton, described by Watson as a "lean-jawed pike" (*The Hound of the Baskervilles*); to say nothing of Holmes's friend and informant, Langdale Pike ("The Adventure of Three Gables").

2 tablespoons breadcrumbs
1 cup heavy cream
2 egg yolks
5 stems of dill, or 1 teaspoon dried dill
4 tomatoes (8 ounces)
1 whole lemon
4 sprigs watercress

1) Eviscerate the pike and scale it. Rinse it with cold water, and dry it with a towel.

2) Slice the onions thinly.

3) Heat 2 ounces of the butter and sauté the onions for 10 minutes or until they are a golden brown. Season them with salt and pepper.

4) Line a roasting pan with aluminum foil, and pour the onion and fat into the centre.

5) Season the pike inside and outside with salt and set it on top of the onions.

6) Mix 2 ounces of the butter with the anchovy paste and flake it over the pike. Then sprinkle it with the lemon peel cut into *julienne* strips. Top it with breadcrumbs.

7) Close the aluminum foil with a twist. Bake it in a preheated 350° to 375°F. oven for 20 minutes.

8) Make the sauce by mixing the heavy cream, egg yolks, and dill. Season it with salt to taste.

9) Open the aluminum foil, and pour the sauce around the pike. Roast it open for 10 minutes or more.

10) Wash the tomatoes and cut them into halves. Top each tomato half with a flake of butter and broil for 3 to 4 minutes.

11) Wash the lemon and cut it into wedges.

12) Garnish the pike with the tomatoes, lemon, and watercress.

☞ Parsley Potatoes[3]

Serves 4 to 6

1 pound new potatoes
½ teaspoon salt, or to taste

---

[3] The noble spud was to be praised by Holmes in a subsequent adventure: "With a spud, a tin box, and an elementary book on botany, there are instructive days to be spent." ("The Adventure of Wisteria Lodge.")

2 ounces butter
1 to 2 tablespoons chopped parsley

1) Boil the potatoes.
2) Peel them and season them with salt.
3) Melt the butter; add the chopped parsley.
4) Fold the butter and parsley into the potatoes.
5) Serve them right away.

☞ **White Wine Sherbet**

Serves 4 to 6

2½ cups sugar
¾ cup water
Juice of 2 lemons
Juice of 1 orange
2 cups white wine[4]
2 egg whites

1) Over low heat, make a syrup with 2 cups plus 3 tablespoons of the sugar and the water.

2) Cool the syrup, then add it to the juice of the lemons and the orange.

3) Strain the syrup and add the wine.

4) Check the sugar content with the floating egg test: Place a whole uncooked egg (in the shell) in the liquid. If the proportion of ingredients is correct for a white wine sherbet, the top of the egg, about the size of a quarter, will show through the top of the liquid. If the egg does not rise this far, add more sugar. If it rises too far, add more water.

5) Pour the liquid into ice trays and place it in the freezer.

6) Add just enough water to the remaining 5 tablespoons of sugar to dissolve it, and heat it gently in the top of a double boiler until it becomes a syrup.

7) Beat the egg whites to a froth; pour the boiling syrup into them, and continue whisking until the mixture is completely cool. Gently mix this meringue mixture into the first frozen mixture. Serve it in chilled glasses.

Sherbets or ices were commonly served between courses to refresh the palate.

---

[4] Montrachet is a white wine of established Canonicity ("The Adventure of the Veiled Lodger"), but any white wine may be used.

☞ Wild Duck the Hunter's Way

Serves 4 to 6

2 small ducklings (1 to 2 pounds each)[5]
½ lemon
2 to 3 teaspoons salt, or to taste
2 teaspoons crushed peppercorns, or to taste
3 ounces butter
½ cup water
⅓ cup diced carrots
⅓ cup diced onions
⅓ cup diced celery
1 clove garlic
1 teaspoon tomato paste
2 to 3 tablespoons flour
1 to 2 cups beer or ale

1) Clean the ducks, wash them well, and dry them thoroughly inside and outside.

2) Rub the ducks with lemon inside and outside. Season the ducks with salt and pepper, and truss them with a needle on a string.

3) Melt the butter in a roasting pan. Add the ducks, turn them in the butter, add ½ cup of water, and roast them for 40 minutes.

4) Add the diced carrots, onions, celery, and garlic, and roast them for 40 minutes more or until the ducks are done.

5) Remove the ducks from the oven and pan and keep them warm.

6) Add the tomato paste to the vegetables in the pan and brown them for 3 to 5 minutes.

7) Add the flour, and brown it in the oven for 3 to 5 minutes more.

8) Add the beer or ale and cook on top of the stove until the liquid is reduced by ⅓.

9) Season the sauce well and strain it.

10) Cut the ducks in half, remove all bones, and cover them with the sauce.

---

[5] A 3- to 4-pound domestic duck may be substituted without changing anything else in the recipe. Wild duck is risky for the novice, in that if the bird is too old, it is thoroughly unpalatable. Many a hunter has seen his precious quarry discarded when it was discovered that it was too oily to be fit even for the stewpot. Because Holmes was hunting in July, we presume that he and the Trevors pursued the flappers, young wild ducks that had reached adult size but had not yet begun to fly.

☞ Sugared Orange Slices[6]

Dip the oranges briefly in a boiling solution of 2 parts water and 1 part vinegar in order to remove the chemicals with which the rind is usually treated. Rinse them with cold water, and dry them well. Cut each orange in half, and slice the orange halves in slices ⅓ inch thick. Turn them in granulated sugar, and serve them.

☞ Buttered String Beans

Serves 4

1 pound string beans
⅓ to ½ teaspoon salt, or to taste
2 ounces butter
2 to 3 tablespoons breadcrumbs

1) Clean the string beans, washing them well.
2) Bring 2 to 3 quarts of water to a boil. Add the salt.
3) Add the beans and simmer them for 5 to 10 minutes or until they are *al dente*.
4) Drain them well and shock them with cold water.
5) Brown the butter. Add the beans, and sauté them for 2 to 3 minutes. Add the breadcrumbs and sauté them for 2 to 3 minutes more. Season them with salt and serve.

☞ Strawberry Torte

Serves 8

1 pint strawberries
1 cup flour
1½ tablespoons cornstarch
2 egg yolks
3 tablespoons sugar

---

[6] Little did Holmes know, at the dawn of his career, the significance that oranges would later have for him. After September of 1887 (the date of "The Five Orange Pips"), Holmes could never see oranges without a pang of regret that although he solved the mystery, he was unable to save his client's life.

1 tablespoon rum[7]
A pinch of salt
½ cup butter
Flour to dust
4 egg whites
4–5 tablespoons vanilla sugar (or 4–5 tablespoons sugar plus 2
    or 3 drops vanilla extract)
Powdered sugar

1) Wash the strawberries with cold water. Remove the stems and dry them well.

2) Mix the flour and cornstarch together, and fold the egg yolks, sugar, rum, and salt into the mixture.

3) Cut the butter into flakes, and work it in from the outside of the dough to the inside until the dough is smooth. Cool it for 30 minutes.

4) Dust the counter top with flour, and roll the dough into the size of the mould you will use.

5) Put the dough into a spring mould or pie plate, pierce it with a fork, and bake it in a preheated 350° to 375°F. oven for 15 minutes.

6) Whip the egg whites with vanilla sugar (or sugar plus vanilla) until they are stiff, then fold in strawberries.

7) Remove the pie shell from the oven. Fill it with the meringue mixture.

8) Put it back into the oven and bake it at 350° to 375°F. for 20 minutes.

9) Dust with powdered sugar.

The Pheasant Months

Sherlock Holmes, by his own admission, had few friends in college. Other than Victor Trevor, Holmes's only known acquaintance was the aristocratic Reginald Musgrave of "The Musgrave Ritual," who, like Trevor, was to become a client of the youthful Sherlock Holmes. It was Musgrave

[7] Rum, a favourite drink of sailors, is always appropriate to a seafaring story. The *Gloria Scott* was an ill-fated ship bound from England to Australia. Later in Holmes's career, rum was an important clue to the murder of former sea captain Peter Cary ("The Adventure of Black Peter").

who gave the impetus for the following menu, from a house party during pheasant season which, regrettably, Holmes did not attend. Social occasions never really interested the Master, and after he began his career as a consulting detective, he had time to hunt little but the criminal.

Reginald Musgrave was descended from one of the very oldest and most distinguished families in the kingdom. In the sixteenth century the Musgrave family "had established itself in western Sussex, where the Manor House of Hurlstone is perhaps the oldest inhabited building in the country." There young Musgrave, after his father's death, took up the management of this ancient estate. He kept a large staff, for, as he described Hurlstone, "it is a rambling place and takes a good deal of looking after . . . and in the pheasant months I usually have a house-party, so that it would not do to be short handed."

It was about the disappearance of one of these servants, the butler Brunton, that Musgrave had sought the aid of his former college acquaintance. During the course of this adventure, Holmes solved the mystery, uncovering circumstances that extended back in time almost to the sixteenth-century origins of Hurlstone itself.

We have chosen to present a menu from one of Reginald Musgrave's house parties at the time that the exceptional butler, Brunton, was in service at Hurlstone. During those years it was said of him by Musgrave, "The butler of Hurlstone is always a thing that is remembered by all who visit us."

The role of the butler in a household is as ancient and honourable as Hurlstone itself. The word "butler" is derived from "Bottler," for the original duty of this servant was to bottle the wine. This work could only be part-time, and so the bottler was asked to serve at meals. He was not particularly skilled at this line of work, however, so he merely brought in a large tray and let the diners help themselves. Through the ages, his role in the dining room and ultimately in the entire household evolved into ever increasing importance until he managed the entire staff. The original character of the role of bottler was preserved, however, in the butler's usual responsibility for the wine cellar.

It is in the honour of the profession of the late, lamented Brunton and his part in the beginning of Holmes's career, therefore, that this meal from the pheasant months is proposed:

> Artichoke Tartare
> Onion Soup Hurlstone
> Fish Roulade with Sauce Piquant
> Lemon Ice
> Breast of Pheasant with Grapes
> Corn Sticks
> Pear Compote with Red Wine

☞ **Artichoke Tartare**

Serves 4 to 8

½ pound chopped beef
1 small onion, finely chopped
½ to 1 teaspoon salt, or to taste
4 grinds pepper, or to taste
Fresh parsley, chopped
1 egg
8 artichoke bottoms (use canned ones, or prepare them using the recipe given below for boiled artichokes)
8 teaspoons grated Parmesan cheese

1) Mix the chopped beef with the finely diced onion. Season it well with salt and pepper and a little chopped parsley. Add the egg.

2) Dry the artichoke bottoms and stuff them with the meat mixture.

3) Top them with the Parmesan cheese.

4) Bake them in a preheated 375° to 400° F. oven for 5 minutes.
This dish may be eaten either hot or cold.

BOILED ARTICHOKES

1) Trim the artichokes, cut off the stems at their base, and cut off the spiky leaf tops. Round each leaf with scissors.

2) Wash the artichokes and put them into enough boiling water so that they will float.

3) Cook them at a rolling boil. The cooking time will be from 25 to 45 minutes, depending upon the size and quality of the artichokes.

4) Test for whether the artichokes are fully cooked by putting a fork into the bottom of one of them. If the fork meets no resistance, and the leaves may be easily removed, the artichoke is done. To use the artichoke bottom, remove the leaves and prickly center of the artichoke. It is the privilege of the cook to enjoy the leaf bases.

☞ **Onion Soup Hurlstone**

Serves 4 to 8

1 pound onions
3 ounces butter

2 tablespoons flour
6 to 7 cups meat stock
2 egg yolks
2 tablespoons water
1½ to 3 teaspoons salt, or to taste
⅓ teaspoon pepper, or to taste
2 tablespoons white wine
½ cup heavy cream
4 slices white bread
1 tablespoon each of chives, sorrel, and dill

1) Peel the onions and cut them into fine slices or *julienne*.
2) Sauté the onions with the butter until they are transparent.
3) Dust them with flour, and cook them for 2 to 3 minutes more.
4) Add the meat stock and boil for 20 minutes.
5) Mix the egg yolks with the 2 tablespoons of water; add the salt, pepper, white wine, and cream.
6) Remove the soup from the fire. Fold the egg mixture into the soup, and adjust the seasoning.
7) Cut the bread slices into small cubes and toast them.
8) Chop the herbs finely.
9) Pour the soup into a tureen; sprinkle it with the croutons and herbs, and serve.

☞ Fish Roulades with Sauce Piquant[1]

Serves 4

20 ounces fish fillet (Boston sole or flounder)
A little lemon juice or vinegar
½ teaspoon salt

Sauce Piquant:
2 ounces diced bacon
1 medium-sized onion, diced
12 tablespoons canned milk
Juice of 1 lemon
2 to 3 diced pickles
2 teaspoons mustard
⅓ teaspoon sugar

---

[1] Had the unfortunate Brunton not found the ancient ritual of the Musgraves to be piquant, he would never have come to grief, and Holmes would never have been consulted in this case.

Salt and pepper to taste
1 tablespoon cornstarch
Madeira wine
1½ ounces grated mild Cheddar cheese
A little butter

1) Rinse the fish fillet, dry it well, sprinkle ¾ of the lemon juice over it, and marinate it for ½ hour. Season it with salt.

2) Form the fish into small roulades and secure each with a toothpick; set the roulades into a buttered pan.

3) Prepare the Sauce Piquant: Sauté the bacon. When it is brown, add the onion and sauté it until it is golden brown. Allow the bacon mixture to cool.

4) Mix the canned milk with the remaining lemon juice, the cold bacon mixture, pickles, mustard, and sugar. Season the mixture with salt and pepper.

5) Mix the cornstarch with just enough Madeira wine to liquefy it. Mix it with the above mixture and bring to a boil.

6) Pour the sauce mixture over the fish rolls. Sprinkle them with cheese and butter flakes. Bake for 25 to 35 minutes at 350° to 400° F.

Note: If sauce is too thin, thicken with cornstarch.

☞ Lemon Ice

Serves 4

2 cups water
Juice of 3 to 4 lemons
1½ cups sugar

1) Combine the water, lemon juice, and sugar.

2) Test the sugar content with the floating egg test: Drop a raw egg (in the shell) into the bowl containing the sugar mixture. If the proportion of sugar is correct for a lemon ice, the tip of the egg, about the size of a quarter, will show through the top of the liquid. If the egg does not float, add more sugar. If too much of the egg shows, add more liquid.

3) Pour into freezer trays and freeze.

☞ Breast of Pheasant with Grapes

Serves 4

2 oven-ready pheasants (2 pounds each)
1 cup water

½ to 1 teaspoon salt, or to taste
6 ounces green grapes
6 ounces blue grapes
8 slices white bread, grated
1½ ounces butter
¼ to ⅓ cup white wine

1) Rinse the pheasants with cold water and dry them.

2) Bone the pheasants; remove the breasts, and reserve the legs for other uses.

3) Boil the bones and wings in 1 cup of water in a covered pot for 20 minutes. Strain the broth and season it with salt.

4) Heat 4 ounces of green grapes and 4 ounces of blue grapes in the pheasant broth. Drain the grapes and keep them in a warm place. Reserve the broth.

5) Cut the pheasant breasts lengthwise 1 or 2 times. Season with salt, and roll them in breadcrumbs.

6) Heat the butter and brown the pheasant breasts on each side for ½ minute. Then cook them for 6 minutes on each side. Baste them continually with butter during the cooking.

7) Remove the meat and deglaze the pan with wine and pheasant broth.

8) Heat the grapes again, and arrange them with the meat on a silver tray.

9) Garnish the tray with the remaining fresh grapes, and serve the sauce on the side.

☞ Corn Sticks

Serves 4 to 6

5 cups water
½ teaspoon salt
1½ cups cornmeal
1 to 2 ounces butter

1) Combine the water, salt, and cornmeal. Cook it in a heavy pot, covered, in a 350° F. oven for ½ hour or until it is done. It is sufficiently cooked when the mixture comes away from the sides of the pan when it is stirred with a spoon.

2) Remove it from the oven. Fold in the butter, and pour it into a slightly buttered baking tray to cool.

3) When it is cool, cut it into small sticks, and sauté them in butter until they are golden brown. Serve them hot.

☞ **Pear Compote with Red Wine**

Serves 4

    1 pound small pears[2]
    ½ cup sugar
    1 cup water
    2 cups red wine
    1 tablespoon cornstarch

  1) Wash, peel, and core the pears.

  2) Bring the sugar, water, and wine to a boil.

  3) Add the pears to the wine broth, and simmer them over a low fire for 30 minutes.

  4) Remove the pears with a slotted spoon.

  5) Mix the cornstarch with a little cold water and add to the wine mixture; bring to a boil and pour over the pears.

  6) Cool the pears and keep them refrigerated until serving time.

A Cold Supper in Kent

Cold meals best suited Holmes when he was actively sleuthing. No one could predict when he would finish his investigating (or his contemplating) and be ready for nourishment. Mrs. Neville St. Clair, his client in "The Man with the Twisted Lip," understood this clearly when the Detective stayed at her home in Kent. Her husband had disappeared, having been last seen in an opium den, the Bar of Gold. Foul play was suspected.

Holmes pursued the case both in London and at the St. Clairs' home in Kent. On one occasion he returned to Kent to spend the night and un-

---

[2] To commemorate Holmes's success in resolving "the famous card scandal of the Nonpareil Club" (referred to in *The Hound of the Baskervilles*) the tart, autumn-ripening French pear called *nonpareille* may be used. It is similar to the pear known in the United States as Bosc, which may be taken, in turn, to commemorate "The Boscombe Valley Mystery."

expectedly brought Dr. Watson with him. Mrs. St. Clair was evidently disappointed that Holmes's companion was not her husband, but she welcomed the travellers graciously: "I am delighted to see you. . . . You will I am sure forgive anything which may be wanting in our arrangements." She then led her guests into "a well-lit dining room upon the table of which a cold supper had been laid out."

One commentator has suggested that Mrs. St. Clair was indeed grieved to see that it was Watson who accompanied Holmes to spend the night.[1] And he slyly conjectured that Mrs. St. Clair would have been crestfallen to see anyone at all join the Master for the overnight stay. Sherlockians, of course, never miss an opportunity to embroil Holmes in some romantic adventure, and some efforts, it may be said, have rested on far less evidence than this one. Consider her greeting, which, by the way, was offered while she was dressed—as a bereaved wife—in *mousseline-de-soie,* not to mention pink chiffon: "The door flew open and there she stood with her figure outlined against the flood of light, one hand raised in eagerness, her body slightly bent, her head and face protruded, with eager eyes and parted lips, a standing question."

If she was a designing woman, and if, the suggestion follows, Holmes brought Watson as a chaperone, it was so much the better for Watson, for the meal, we infer, was an entirely enticing repast. We have endeavoured to reconstruct a suitable menu, but the dessert leaves nothing to doubt. During the course of the conversation, Holmes exclaimed, "It is, of course, a trifle . . . there is nothing so important as trifles."

> Soused Mackerel
> Potted Shrimp[2]
> Cold Jellied Beef
> English Cucumber Salad
> Potato Salad
> Trifle

☞ Soused Mackerel in White Wine

Serves 10 to 12

    4 one-pound fresh mackerels
    1 large onion, sliced

[1] Richard Asher, "Holmes and the Fair Sex," *Sherlock Holmes Journal,* Summer, 1955, 2, pp. 15–22.

[2] The mackerel is soused and the shrimp potted as a reminder of the intoxicated state of the patrons of the Bar of Gold.

　　1 tablespoon chopped parsley, plus some sprigs for garnish
　　2 bay leaves
　　1 teaspoon peppercorns
　　1 teaspoon salt
　　2 cups dry white wine
　　2 tablespoons lemon juice

　　1) Eviscerate the fish, discard the heads, and wash the mackerels thoroughly.

　　2) Place the fish in a baking pan; sprinkle them with the onion slices, 1 tablespoon of chopped parsley, bay leaves, peppercorns, and salt.

　　3) Pour the wine and the lemon juice over the fish and bring it to a boil over medium heat.

　　4) Cover it and bake it in a 350° F. oven for 15 to 20 minutes. Cool it at room temperature, and allow it to cool for several hours more in the refrigerator.

　　5) Debone the mackerels and arrange them on a serving platter.

　　6) Strain the cooking liquid over the fillets and decorate them with sprigs of parsley.

☞ Potted Shrimp

Serves 10 to 12

　　8 ounces Lobster Butter (see recipe below), or 8 ounces butter plus
　　　½ teaspoon paprika
　　2 cups cooked and shelled titi (tiny) shrimp
　　¼ teaspoon mace
　　¼ teaspoon cayenne pepper
　　1 to 2 tablespoons lemon juice

　　1) Melt the lobster butter (or butter plus paprika) in a saucepan.

　　2) Add the shrimp and the seasonings and simmer them for 5 minutes.

　　3) Add the lemon juice, and pour the mixture into a soufflé mould or individual ramekins.

　　4) Chill it for 2 hours before serving.

LOBSTER BUTTER

Makes 8 ounces of butter

　　2 to 3 ounces lobster coral (the undeveloped eggs of a lobster)
　　7 ounces butter

1) Chop the lobster coral and work it into the butter.
2) Melt the butter mixture and bring it to a boil.
3) Cool the butter and allow it to rest overnight in the refrigerator.
4) Pour off the water that has collected, and remelt the butter.
5) Pour the lobster butter into a crock and keep it in the refrigerator or freezer. It will keep indefinitely in the freezer.

☞ Cold Jellied Beef in a Casserole

Serves 10

½ pound fat back, cut into sticks
1 to 1½ tablespoons salt
1 teaspoon peppercorns, crushed
½ to 1 teaspoon thyme
2 to 3 bay leaves, crushed
2 tablespoons chopped parsley
3 pounds beef (top round)
¼ cup whiskey
½ bottle red wine
2 shallots, chopped
¼ pound fresh pork rind
1 calf's foot (optional)
½ pound lean slab bacon
4 large onions
4 cloves garlic
4 carrots
3½ tablespoons butter
½ pound bacon slices
1 cup flour
⅓ cup water

1) Season the fat-back sticks with some of the salt and pepper. Roll them in a little of the thyme, 1 crushed bay leaf and ½ teaspoon of parsley and allow them to rest for 1 hour.
2) Cut the beef into 1- to 1½-inch pieces. Lard them with the fat back, working with the grain of the meat.
3) Sprinkle the larded beef with salt, pepper, and more of the herbs. Place it in a casserole together with the whiskey, red wine, chopped shallots, and remaining chopped parsley. Marinate it for 2 hours.
4) Put the pork rind and calf's foot into 3 to 4 cups cold water. Bring it to a boil, and boil it for 45 minutes. Cool it in cold water, and cut the rind into small squares. Break the bone from the calf's foot and discard it.

5) Cut the slab bacon into large dice, and scald it in the water in which the rind was cooked. The water may be reserved and used as stock for the casserole.

6) Dice the onions, mash the garlic, and slice the carrots thinly.

7) Drain and dry the pieces of larded beef, reserving the marinade. Heat the butter in a skillet, and brown the meat, 5 to 6 pieces at a time.

8) Line a large casserole with bacon slices. The bacon slices should over-lap so that the entire casserole is covered. Add one-third of the meat, carrots, onions, and garlic, then half of the pork rind and bacon pieces. Season with salt and half of the remaining herbs. Add a second layer of meat, vegetables, the rest of the herbs, a layer of pork rind and bacon, and finally the last layer of meat and vegetables.

9) Pour in the reserved marinade and stock (the water in which the bacon was scalded or any other stock).

10) Cover the casserole with a lid. Mix 1 cup flour and ⅓ cup water together to make a paste. Dust counter top with a little flour. Roll the paste into a long, thin cigar shape. Brush the edge of the casserole top with water, and press the roll of flour-and-water paste into place to seal the edge.

11) Bake in the oven at a low heat (200° to 225°F.) for 6 hours.

12) Remove the cover. Skim off the fat, and cool the casserole. Serve it cold.

☞ English Cucumber Salad

Serves 10 to 12

    7 cucumbers (28 to 32 ounces)
    1½ cups mayonnaise
    3 teaspoons chopped chives
    ½ cup white vinegar
    1 to 1½ teaspoons salt
    4 grinds of pepper
    1 onion, finely diced
    ½ cup oil

1) Peel the cucumbers and slice them thinly.

2) Combine the mayonnaise, chives, vinegar, salt, pepper, and onion and add them to the cucumbers. Mix the ingredients well.

3) Allow the mixture to rest for 30 minutes. Adjust the seasoning, then add the oil.

☞ Potato Salad

Serves 10 to 12

2 pounds potatoes
¼ to ⅓ cup vinegar
⅓ cup hot chicken stock
⅓ cup diced onion
½ to 1 teaspoon coarse (Kosher) salt
⅓ teaspoon pepper
⅓ teaspoon sugar
½ cup diced apples
1 teaspoon chives
¼ cup oil

1) Wash the potatoes and cook them in their jackets.

2) When they are done, cool them slightly and peel them while they are still warm. Dice or slice them.

3) Mix the vinegar, stock, onions, salt, pepper, sugar, apples, and chives, then mix with the potatoes. Taste and adjust the seasoning. Then add the oil and mix well.

4) Allow the salad to rest for 1 to 2 hours before serving.

☞ Trifle

Serves 10 to 12

1 Pound Cake (see recipe, page 154)
½ cup raspberry jam
1 cup sliced almonds
¾ cup sugar
½ cup brandy
½ cup dry sherry
2 cups heavy cream
2 tablespoons superfine sugar
2 cups fresh or frozen raspberries
3 cups Custard Sauce (see recipe below)

1) Cut the pound cake into ½-inch-thick slices and spread the jam over the slices.

2) Arrange the slices in a glass serving bowl. Sprinkle the almonds over each layer.

3) Dissolve the sugar in the brandy and the sherry; heat until the sugar is completely dissolved. Cool the syrup and pour over the pound cake.

4) Whip the cream until stiff, and add the superfine sugar.

5) Scatter the raspberries over the cake, saving a dozen for decoration at the end. Spread the custard over the top.

6) Pipe the whipped cream all around the cake and decorate with the remaining raspberries.

A TRIFLING CUSTARD SAUCE

> ½ stick vanilla bean
> 1½ cups boiled milk
> 1 cup granulated sugar
> 7 egg yolks
> 2 tablespoons unflavoured gelatine (2 packages)
> ½ cup heavy cream
> ⅓ cup confectioners' sugar
> 2 teaspoons vanilla sugar (1 package), or 2 teaspoons sugar plus 2 to 3 drops vanilla extract

1) Place the vanilla bean in the boiled milk to steep.

2) Mix the granulated sugar and egg yolks in a saucepan.

3) Dilute the gelatine with some of the milk in which the vanilla bean has been steeped. Dilute the sugar and egg yolks with the rest of the milk.

4) Combine the gelatine and the egg-and-sugar mixture.

5) Put this preparation on a mild fire, preferably in the top of a double boiler, stirring often. *Do not let it boil!*

6) When it is thick enough to coat a spoon that has been withdrawn from the mixture, strain it into a bowl.

7) Cool it, stirring from time to time. When it begins to thicken, whip the heavy cream, and add it along with the powdered sugar and vanilla sugar to the cooled mixture.

Note: If the sauce does not thicken, add 1 to 2 tablespoons of cornstarch.

POUND CAKE

This is the recipe which has given this cake its name, for it calls for a pound of everything. We offer it despite the fact that pound cake is one thing that is far more economical to buy than to make.

1 pound butter (2 cups)
1 pound sugar (2 cups)
1 pound eggs (2 cups) or 8 to 10 whole eggs
1 pound flour (4 cups)
¼ teaspoon baking powder

1) Cream the butter and sugar together. Add the eggs gradually, and fold in the flour and baking powder.

2) Line 2 loaf pans with greased waxed paper. Fill them with the dough and bake them in a 300°F. oven for approximately 1 hour, or until done.

Note: This recipe makes 2 pound cakes. One of them is sufficient for the Trifle, but this recipe should not be divided.

To Babble of Green Peas— in Early April?

Mrs. Hudson, the longsuffering landlady at 221B Baker Street, was well accustomed to the eccentricities of her beloved lodgers. Consider, however, the plight of a new landlady who took on Mr. Holmes and Dr. Watson as temporary boarders. The anonymous landlady of "The Adventure of the Three Students" in an unnamed university town (Oxford or Cambridge, presumably) experienced the catastrophe in 1895 while Holmes spent some time studying Early English charters. His researches interrupted by an unexpected case, Holmes, as usual, forgot mealtime until he had an opportunity to relax—much later. Exclaimed Holmes, "By Jove! My dear fellow, it is nearly nine, and the landlady babbled of green peas at seven-thirty." Adding with a touch of humour, "What with your eternal tobacco, Watson, and your irregularity at meals, I expect you will get notice to quit, and that I shall share your downfall."

We are pleased to note that they were given their belated dinner, and that no eviction has ever been reported.

This belated meal poses a vexing problem to students of Sherlockian chronology. The landlady babbled of green peas (the only menu item mentioned); yet most clues to the dating of the story point to early April,[1] before green peas would have been in season. Production of green peas in early April was unlikely. Early spring peas, though not very plentiful, begin to produce in late April. The rarity of green peas in early April is well illustrated by the following mid-nineteenth-century quotation: "In a biography, immortal as veracious, an inconsiderable spot in Kent is said to have furnished one of its commonest inns with ducks and green peas before the middle of April *once;* the year should be memorable; no mention is made of exorbitant charges for these forced birds and precocious pulse."[2]

Watson intended to obscure everything that would allow identification either of the university or of the participants in the scandal. With the exception of the year, which is explicitly 1895, he apparently obscured the time of the incident as well.

Be that as it may, we shall take the reference to green peas as accurate, and we have chosen duck as a suitable accompaniment. Other menu items have been added, compatible with either a spring or a summer occurrence, thus leaving the question of the precise chronology to be settled over supper.

Liver *Pâté en Croûte*
Clear Consommé with Pancakes
Duckling with Green Peas
Boiled Brown Rice
Treacle Tart

☞ Liver Pâté en Croûte

Serves 8 to 10

2 slices of white bread
½ cup sherry wine

---

[1] Watson's description of when it grew dark indicates a 6:30 sunset, suggesting, therefore, either early April or September. Because the date is probably within the Oxford or Cambridge term, September is rejected. The wearing of overcoat and gloves is mentioned, something unlikely in midsummer. Furthermore, one of the suspects is training for sports, presumed to occur in April, but this is by no means a certain clue, for W. S. Bristowe ("The Three Students in Limelight, Electric Light and Daylight," *Sherlock Holmes Journal*, Winter, 1956, *3*, pp. 2–5) has noted that the Intervarsity sports were run in July during 1895.

[2] Benson E. Hill, *Popular Cookery: or a Diary of Good Living*, London: A. Hall, Virtue & Co., 1842.

    1 pound calf's liver
    ½ pound lean pork
    2 small onions
    2 tablespoons butter
    2 eggs
    1 to 2 teaspoons salt
    ⅓ teaspoon pepper
    ½ teaspoon *Pâté* Spice (see recipe, p. 119)
    Grated orange rind of ½ to 1 orange
    Short Pastry (see recipe, p. 84)
    1 egg yolk

1) Soak the bread in the sherry wine, then squeeze it.

2) Grind the liver, pork, and onions through the fine blade of a meat grinder (or have a butcher do it).

3) Heat the butter, and sauté the above mixture for 5 minutes.

4) Add the squeezed bread and the eggs, spices, and grated orange rind, and stir them well.

5) Prepare the pastry, and roll it out to ⅓-inch thickness on a floured surface.

6) Line a buttered loaf pan with the dough. Fill it with the meat mixture, and top it with the rest of the dough.

7) Brush it with egg yolk, and pierce it with a fork.

8) Bake it in a preheated oven at 300° to 350°F. for 1 hour.

9) Remove the *pâté* from the oven, unmould it, and let it cool.

☞ **Clear Consomme with Pancakes**

Serves 4

    3 quarts or more cold water
    1 pound lean beef, brisket or shin, cut into cubes
    4 pounds beef bones, cracked
    1 teaspoon salt
    2 carrots
    1 parsnip
    1 rib celery
    3 leeks (white part only)
    1 garlic head, crushed
    1 *bouquet garni* (parsley, chervil, bay leaf)
    2 large onions, cut in half and burnt[3]

---

[3] Burn the cut surfaces by placing them directly on top of the burner of an electric stove until they get black, or impale each onion on a fork and hold it in a gas flame.

1) Put the water, beef, and bones into a deep kettle. Bring it slowly to the boiling point, skim it, and season it with salt and skim it again.

2) Dice the vegetables (carrots, parsnip, celery, and leeks).

3) Add the diced vegetables to the pot together with the whole crushed garlic, the *bouquet garni,* and the burned onions.

4) Bring the broth slowly to the boiling point, skim it, then simmer it slowly for 4 hours, after which time it should be reduced in volume to about 6 cups.

5) At the end of the cooking time, adjust the seasonings, and strain it through a cheesecloth.

PANCAKES

Serves 6 to 8

1 cup milk
1 teaspoon salt
1 teaspoon sugar
½ cup butter
2½ cups all-purpose flour
1 tablespoon vegetable oil
4 eggs
1 cup flat beer
1 teaspoon chopped parsley

1) Heat the milk, salt, sugar, and butter in a saucepan until the butter is melted.

2) Put the flour in a large bowl and make a well in the centre. Pour the oil into the well and add the eggs. Mix well by beating with a wire whisk.

3) Add the milk mixture and stir in the beer.

4) Strain the batter through a fine sieve and add the parsley.

5) Allow the batter to rest for 2 hours in the refrigerator before making the pancakes.

6) Fry the pancakes in a lightly greased pan over fairly high heat. Cool them and cut them into fine strips. Serve them in the soup.

Note: This recipe makes many more pancakes than will be needed for the consommé, but, alas, it is not possible to make that small a quantity of pancakes. Happily, these pancakes keep well in the freezer, and they have multiple uses. Stack them with pieces of waxed paper or plastic wrap between. Wrap them all in a plastic bag and put them in the freezer. They may then be removed in the quantities needed. They thaw quickly when separated.

☞ Duckling with Green Peas

Serves 4

    1 three-pound duck
    1½ ounces butter
    12 cubes of bacon, cut from slab bacon
    12 pearl onions
    ¾ cup white wine
    2 cups Brown Sauce (see recipe below)
    1 to 2 teaspoons salt
    ⅓ teaspoon pepper
    Herbs (parsley, leeks, dill)
    16 ounces young green peas (fresh, frozen, or canned)

1) Truss the duck and brown it slowly in butter. As soon as it is brown, remove it from the pan.

2) Add the onions and bacon cubes to the pan and fry them to a light brown. Add the white wine and brown sauce.

3) Replace the duck in the pan. Season it with salt and pepper, and add a small bunch of herbs (parsley, leeks, dill). Cover it and braise it slowly in a 350°F. oven for 40 to 50 minutes.

4) Add the peas during the braising. If fresh or frozen peas are used, add them to the pan 20 minutes before the end of the cooking time. If canned peas are used, wait until the last 5 minutes of cooking time before adding them.

5) When the duck is cooked, remove the bunch of herbs and skim the fat off the sauce.

BROWN SAUCE

    2 pounds beef, chicken, veal, or pork bones
    ⅓ cup diced carrots
    ⅓ cup diced onions
    ⅓ cup diced celery
    ⅓ cup diced parsnips
    2 tablespoons tomato paste
    ½ cup flour
    2 quarts water (or part water, part beer)
    ½ teaspoon salt

1) Brown the bones in a roasting pan. Add the diced vegetables and brown them slightly. Add the tomato paste, and brown the bones for 10 minutes longer.

2) Dust with flour and bake in a 350° oven for 10 to 20 minutes, or until the flour browns slightly.

3) Fill the pan with the water, and mix the ingredients well. Add the salt, bring the sauce to a boil on top of the stove, cover it, then return it to the oven and simmer it for 1½ to 2 hours. Strain it.

4) If the sauce is too thin, reduce it by cooking on top of the stove.

Note: The brown sauce may be frozen in ice-cube trays and kept in the freezer. If it is in cubes, it can be taken out and used as needed, the rest being returned to the freezer.

☞ Boiled Brown Rice

Serves 4

This is a recipe to use, in defiance of package directions,[4] to produce exceptionally light, fluffy rice. It may be used for either brown or white rice.

　1 cup brown rice
　6 cups water
　1 to 1½ teaspoons salt

1) Wash the rice well.

2) Boil it uncovered in the lightly salted water for 16 to 18 minutes.

3) Rinse in hot water, drain well, cover and allow to rest for a few minutes before serving.

☞ Treacle Tart

Makes one 9-inch pie

　1½ cups English golden syrup, or ¾ cup light and ¾ cup dark
　　　corn syrup
　1½ cups fresh breadcrumbs

---

[4] "We all have our systems."—Sherlock Holmes in "The Adventure of Wisteria Lodge."

    1 tablespoon lemon juice
    ½ teaspoon ground ginger
    2 whole eggs
    1 9-inch unbaked pie shell

1) Combine the syrup, breadcrumbs, lemon juice, ginger, and eggs in a large bowl. Mix all the ingredients well.

2) Pour into the pie shell and bake for 20 to 25 minutes in a 350°F. oven. The tart should be golden brown when done. The treacle tart is usually served with a custard sauce (see A Trifling Custard Sauce, p. 154).

The Ultimate Destiny of a Goose

The "Adventure of the Blue Carbuncle" carries us into the great English tradition of Christmas, a season rich in food as well as good feeling. Although Holmes and Watson doubtless participated in the cheery Yuletide customs, those moments were not recorded in the published tales we know and love. Only once do the stories take us into this season of good cheer, and that was because a mystery was presented at 221B Baker Street in the form of a precious stone lodged in the crop of a Christmas goose.[1]

That particular winter was a solitary one for Mr. Sherlock Holmes. Dr. Watson had deserted the familiar lodgings to enjoy wedded domesticity.[2] This was not destined to be a lonely Holmesian Christmas, for on Christmas morning an honest commissionaire named Peterson came to Baker Street with a perplexing little problem: He had found a battered

---

[1] There has been a minor storm of controversy over whether or not a goose has a crop, but the weight of the evidence, empirical and otherwise, favours the existence of a crop. See Ernest Bloomfield Zeisler, "A Pigment of the Imagination," in the *Sherlock Holmes Journal*, Spring, 1961, 5, pp. 50–52, and Editor's Note, *Sherlock Holmes Journal*, Spring, 1961, 5, pp. 35–36.

[2] Most critics agree that this was Dr. Watson's first marriage, and that his wife was Mary Morstan, whom he met during *The Sign of Four*. William Baring-Gould, however, has decided that "The Adventure of the Blue Carbuncle" antedates *The Sign of Four*, making it necessary to invent another first marriage for the good doctor. (*The Annotated Sherlock Holmes*, New York: Clarkson N. Potter, 1967, I, p. 451.)

felt hat and a "most unimpeachable Christmas goose": Would Holmes locate the rightful owner?

In a characteristic tour de force, the Detective discerned a few distinctive features from the hat and bird. The owner of the goose, one Henry Baker, ". . . was highly intellectual, fairly well-to-do within the last three years, although he has now fallen upon evil days. He had foresight, but has less now than formerly, pointing to a moral retrogression, which, when taken with the decline of his fortunes, seems to indicate some evil influence, probably drink, at work upon him. This may account also for the obvious fact that his wife has ceased to love him. . . . He has, however, retained some degree of self-respect. . . . He is a man who leads a sedentary life, goes out little, is out of training entirely, is middle-aged, has grizzled hair which he has had cut within the last few days, and which he anoints with lime-cream. Also . . . it is extremely improbable that he has gas laid on in his house."

Poor Henry Baker, having lost his wife's affection, compounded his misery by losing as well the Christmas goose, which might have served as a peace offering.[3] He had to wait until the second day after Christmas for the Yuletide season to brighten, when Sherlock Holmes presented him with a replacement for the one which had been lost.

The faithful Peterson, on the other hand, had two geese with which to celebrate: the one that he and his wife doubtless provided for Christmas, and the other one which formed the basis for the story, and which he carried off two days later "when there were signs that, in spite of the slight frost, it would be well that it should be eaten without unnecessary delay."

We offer, therefore, a festive Christmas menu with two recipes for goose, to honour the extra goose that Peterson had for Christmas and that Holmes had for an adventure:

> Cold Lamb Cutlets—Family Style
> Londonderry Soup
> Fillet of Dover Sole with Tiny Shrimp Sauce
> Roast Goose from the Gamekeeper's Chimney
> Roast Goose with Sage and Onion Stuffing
> Brussels Sprouts with Chestnuts
> Potato Croquettes
> Mixed Endive Salad
> Cheddar Cheese with Port
> Christmas Plum Pudding

[3] This goose, by the way, was described in the Canon as white with a black bar across the tail. S. Tupper Bigelow, after assiduous research, has discovered that no known goose fits that description. "Bar Tailed Geese," in *Sherlock Holmes Journal*, Spring, 1964, *6*, pp. 108–109.

☞ Cold Lamb Cutlets—Family Style

Serves 4

8 lamb cutlets
2 teaspoons dried marjoram
8 small bay leaves
8 slices bacon
Oil
1 teaspoon celery salt
1 teaspoon paprika
Boston lettuce
Lemon juice, salt, and pepper
8 teaspoons mint jelly
4 thin slices of lemon

1) Rub each cutlet with marjoram.

2) Place one bay leaf on each cutlet.

3) Wrap a slice of bacon around each cutlet.

4) Heat 4 tablespoons of oil and sauté the cutlets for 6 minutes on each side, or until they are cooked to the desired doneness.

5) Remove the bacon, and season each cutlet with celery salt and paprika. Allow them to cool.

6) Marinate the leaves of Boston lettuce with oil, lemon juice, salt, and pepper. Cover a platter with them.

7) Set the cutlets on the lettuce leaves. Brush them lightly with mint jelly. Garnish them with lemon slices and serve them with toast and butter.

☞ Londonderry Soup

Serves 4

1 large onion, chopped
1 green pepper, diced
1½ ounces butter
1 knife tip or more of curry
⅓ cup flour
3½ cups veal stock or bouillon
½ to 1 teaspoon salt, if necessary
2 ounces mushrooms
2 teaspoons Madeira wine
1 egg yolk
½ cup heavy cream

1) Sauté the chopped onion and diced pepper in 1 ounce of butter. Season them with curry.

2) Make a roux by adding the flour to the pan and stirring well.

3) Add the bouillon or stock and boil for 20 minutes. Strain the soup and season it with the salt.

4) Slice the mushrooms in the remaining butter; sauté them and add them to the soup. Bring to a boil, and remove from the heat.

5) Add the Madeira wine.

6) Mix together the egg yolk and cream, add a little of the hot liquid to it, and add it to the soup. Taste it, adjust the seasonings, and serve it hot.

☞ Fillet of Dover Sole with Tiny Shrimp[4] Sauce

Serves 4

8 Dover sole fillets (approximately 1½ to 2 ounces each)
Juice of ½ lemon
2 to 3 teaspoons salt
½ teaspoon pepper
⅓ ounce butter to grease the pan
½ cup white wine
2 tablespoons flour
1 cup heavy cream
5 ounces tiny shrimp
5½ ounces fresh mushrooms
2 to 3 dashes Worcestershire sauce

1) Dry the Dover sole fillets with a paper towel.

2) Sprinkle the lemon juice over them and allow them to rest for 10 minutes. Season them with salt and pepper.

3) Roll them up, and fasten each roll with a toothpick.

4) Grease a fireproof dish with butter and set the fillets into it. Pour the wine over the fish and cover the dish with a lid.

5) Cook them in a preheated 350° to 400°F. oven for 10 minutes. Prepare the sauce while the fish is cooking.

6) Whip heavy cream into the flour until it is smooth.

7) Heat it slowly, stirring constantly until it thickens.

8) Add the tiny shrimp.

---

[4] When Sherlock Holmes confronted the thief, Ryder, at the conclusion of this adventure, he exclaimed, "What a shrimp it is, to be sure."

9) Wash and slice the mushrooms and add them to the sauce mixture.

10) Cook the sauce for 15 minutes over a slow fire. Season it with the Worcestershire sauce.

11) Remove the fireproof dish from the oven and pour the fish stock carefully into a small dish. Stir the fish stock slowly into the shrimp sauce. If it is too thin, reduce it to syrup thickness. Taste it and adjust the seasoning.

12) Pour the sauce over the fish and bake it for 5 more minutes at 350° to 400°F.

☞ **Roast Goose from the Gamekeeper's Chimney**

Serves 4 to 6

1 oven-ready goose (6 to 7 pounds)
Salt and pepper to taste
Juice of ½ lemon
1 pound apples
3½ ounces raisins
½ teaspoon dried marjoram
2 cups hot water
8 small apples
½ pound cranberries or lingonberries
1½ ounces butter
1½ cups water
1 tablespoon cornstarch
5 tablespoons cold water
2 to 3 teaspoons salt, or to taste
2 tablespoons heavy cream
3 level tablespoons sugar
½ bunch parsley

1) Rinse the goose with cold water, inside and outside. Dry it with a towel. Season it inside and outside with salt, pepper, and lemon juice.

2) Peel the pound of apples, cut them into quarters, remove the cores, and cut the apples into small pieces.

3) Wash the raisins in a sieve with hot water. Drain them well.

4) Mix the small apple pieces, raisins, and marjoram.

5) Fill the cavity of the goose with this mixture. Close the cavity with a needle and butcher twine.

6) Place the goose in a roasting pan and roast it in a preheated 350°F.

oven for 2 hours and 40 minutes. During the roasting time, pour a little hot water into the pan at short intervals. Baste the goose from time to time during the last 10 minutes of roasting, according to need, in order to make it more crisp.

7) To prepare the garnish, wash the 8 small apples well and dry them. Hollow them out and fill the cavities with the cranberries or lingonberries (some berries should be left over for the sauce). Top them with flakes of butter. Wrap the apples in aluminum foil and place them in the roasting pan around the goose 30 minutes before the end of the roasting time.

8) Remove the goose and the apples and keep them warm.

9) Remove the fat and save it for other uses.[5] Deglaze the roasting pan with 1½ cups of water and pour it into a pot.

10) Mix the cornstarch with a little cold water. Stir it into the hot liquid and bring it to one boil. Remove it from the heat and season it with salt and pepper.

11) Stir in the heavy cream and remaining berries. Heat the sauce thoroughly but do not let it boil.

12) Carve the goose and set it on a warm platter.

13) Remove the aluminum foil from the apples and set the apples around the goose. Sprinkle a little sugar over them. Garnish the platter with some fresh parsley. Serve the sauce separately.

☞ Roast Goose with Sage and Onion Stuffing

Serves 4 to 6

    1 oven-ready goose (6 to 7 pounds)
    ½ cup chopped onions
   10 slices white bread, cubed
    ½ pound finely chopped suet
    1 tablespoon chopped parsley
    ½ teaspoon sage
    1 to 1½ teaspoons salt
    ⅓ teaspoon pepper
    ½ cup diced carrots
    2 eggs

---

[5] Goose fat is appropriate to any of the uses of butter or shortening. In Holmes's time, it was especially valued when lightly salted and spread over toast.

½ cup diced celery
½ cup diced onions
1 to 2 teaspoons tomato paste
1 tablespoon cornstarch
1 can beer (12 ounces)

1) Sauté the onions and allow them to cool.

2) Soak the bread cubes in water and squeeze them out.

3) Mix the chopped suet and the bread well. Add the sautéed onions, parsley, sage, salt, pepper, and eggs. Mix well.

4) Fill the goose with this stuffing and sew it up.

5) Truss the goose and roast it in a moderate oven until both goose and stuffing are cooked (approximately 1¾ to 2 hours in a 350°F. oven).

6) After the goose has been in the oven for about 1 hour, add the diced carrots, celery, and onions to the pan.

7) When the goose is cooked, remove it from the pan and keep it warm.

8) Pour off the fat and reserve it for other uses.

9) Add 1 to 2 teaspoons of tomato paste to the pan in which the goose was cooked and brown it slightly in the oven.

10) Dilute 1 tablespoon of cornstarch with a little beer and set it aside.

11) Add the rest of the beer to the pan and boil it for 8 to 10 minutes.

12) Taste it and adjust the seasoning.

13) Thicken the sauce with the diluted cornstarch. Strain it and serve it separately.

☞ Brussels Sprouts with Chestnuts[6]

Serves 4

½ pound chestnuts
5 cups water
1 tablespoon sugar
2 ounces butter
2 cups hot meat broth
1½ pounds Brussels sprouts
½ teaspoon salt, if necessary
A pinch of grated nutmeg

[6] The mention of chestnuts recalls two lovely women of the Canon, described as having chestnut-coloured hair: Lucy Ferrier of *A Study in Scarlet* and Violet Hunter of "The Adventure of the Copper Beeches."

1) Cut the chestnuts crosswise. Boil them in 1 cup of water for 15 minutes. Remove them from the water and peel them.

2) Heat the sugar with 1½ ounces of butter until it caramelizes.

3) Add the chestnuts and the meat broth and simmer them for 15 minutes.

4) Remove the chestnuts and reduce the broth to the consistency of syrup. Add the chestnuts again and sauté them until they are brown.

5) Wash the Brussels sprouts and cut the stems crosswise. Place them in 4 cups of boiling salted water. Cook them for 15 minutes or until they are *al dente*. (If frozen Brussels sprouts are used, follow package directions.) Season them with nutmeg and drain them.

6) Add the cooked Brussels sprouts to the chestnuts; add the rest of the butter and serve them.

☞ Potato Croquettes

Serves 4 to 6

2 pounds potatoes
1 ounce butter or margarine
3 egg yolks or 2 whole eggs
3 tablespoons flour
A pinch of nutmeg
A pinch of salt
2 whole eggs
4 cups breadcrumbs
Oil or vegetable shortening

1) Wash and peel the potatoes. Boil them in salted water until they are soft.

2) Drain them and set them in a warm oven for 1 to 5 minutes, to remove the steam.

3) Mash the potatoes through a sieve or potato press.

4) Stir in the butter, 3 egg yolks or 2 whole eggs, the flour, nutmeg, and salt. Mix them well until they are smooth.

5) Dust a surface with flour, and form the potatoes into long rolls. Cut the rolls into 1- to 2-inch pieces.

6) Whip 2 whole eggs and mix them with 3 tablespoons of water; dip

the potato rolls into the mixture. Roll them in breadcrumbs and allow them to rest for ½ hour.

7) Fry them in oil until they are brown.

☞ Mixed Endive Salad

Serves 4 to 6

1 head curly endive
4 to 6 small tomatoes
2 pimientos or red peppers
½ bunch watercress
2 hard-cooked eggs
1 egg yolk (uncooked)
8 tablespoons oil
4 tablespoons vinegar
1 teaspoon mustard
½ teaspoon white pepper
1 teaspoon finely chopped capers
2 tablespoons chopped parsley
2 tablespoons red wine

1) Remove the outer leaves of the endive and cut the remainder into *julienne* strips. Wash and drain them well.

2) Cut the tomatoes into 8 wedges and the pimientos into *julienne* strips. Remove the leaves from the cress.

3) Make the dressing by mincing the hard-cooked egg yolks and mixing them with the uncooked yolk, oil, vinegar, mustard, white pepper, capers, parsley, and red wine. Chop the cooked egg white and add it.

4) Mix all the salad ingredients with the dressing.

☞ Christmas Plum Pudding

To be in time for Christmas, one should begin making the plum pudding about a month ahead of time. This English specialty needs to age for a couple of days before it is cooked, and it needs to age a minimum of three weeks afterwards. Because the recipe calls for many ingredients, and requires long cooking and marination times, it appears to be more difficult than it really is. The recipe is not as difficult as it looks, and the result is well worth the effort. As to the long time during which it must marinate, we give the advice of Sherlock Holmes: "No short cuts. Things must be done . . . in order."[7]

Serves 4 to 6

6 slices stale white bread
5½ ounces beef suet (kidney fat)
3½ ounces raisins
3½ ounces dried currants
1¾ ounces candied citron or lemon
1¾ ounces candied cherries
1 tart apple (5½ ounces)
2½ ounces chopped almonds
Grated peel of 2 oranges
Grated peel of 1 lemon
10 level tablespoons flour (2½ ounces)
11 level tablespoons sugar (5½ ounces)
1 knife tip ground cinnamon
1 knife tip ground ginger
1 knife tip ground cloves
1 knife tip ground nutmeg
½ teaspoon salt
3 eggs
Juice of 1 lemon
Juice of 1 orange
½ cup brandy
½ cup sherry
12 lumps sugar
2 tablespoons brandy

1) Grate the white bread finely.
2) Remove the skin from the kidney fat and grind or grate it finely.
3) Soak the raisins and currants for 5 minutes in hot water. Drain and dry them well.
4) Chop the candied citron and cherries coarsely.
5) Peel the apple and grate it.
6) Put all the above items in a large bowl.
7) Combine the chopped almonds, orange and lemon peel, flour, sugar, spices, and salt, and fold them into the first mixture. Mix well.

---

[7] "The Adventure of the Retired Colourman."

8) Break the eggs into the mixture. Add the lemon and orange juice, and work it together well either by hand or by machine.

9) Work the brandy and sherry into the mixture.

10) Put the doughlike mixture into a stone or pottery crock and allow it to rest, refrigerated, for 48 hours.

11) Lightly grease a china pudding mould or a 2½-pint Pyrex bowl. Put the dough in the mould. Cover it with greased waxed or parchment paper.

12) Grease the center of a large dishtowel or piece of cheesecloth. Dust it with flour, stretch it tightly over the top of the mould on top of the waxed paper, and tie the ends securely around the side of the mould.

13) Put the mould on a trivet in a large pot.

14) Fill the pot with boiling water, enough to reach three-fourths of the way up the side of the mould.

15) Boil the plum pudding for 6 hours. Add boiling water as needed in order to keep a constant water level.

16) Remove the mould from the pot and allow it to cool to room temperature.

17) Remove the cloth and the paper. Unmould the pudding and wrap it in greased aluminum foil. Make sure that the pudding is well covered.

18) Allow it to rest in the refrigerator or other cool place for a minimum of 3 weeks.

19) Before serving it, return the pudding to the mould. Cover it tightly with a lid or aluminum foil, set it in a pan of water, and cook it again for 2 hours. (This may be done in the oven. If it is heated on top of the stove, be sure to put the mould on a trivet in the pan of water.)

20) Unmould the pudding on a tray and top it with lumps of sugar.

21) Warm 2 tablespoons of brandy lightly; pour it over the sugar on the pudding and ignite it.[8] Serve the pudding flaming.

Plum pudding may be served with a variety of sweet sauces. We recommend hot apricot brandy sauce.

HOT APRICOT BRANDY SAUCE

1 jar (10 ounces) apricot jam
⅓ cup brandy

Mix the jam and brandy together and heat them gently, stirring occasionally.

---

[8] Holmes needed brandy in order to revive the pitiful villain, Ryder, at the conclusion of "The Adventure of the Blue Carbuncle."

The Game Is Afoot

"... we will begin another investigation, in which, also, a bird will be the chief feature."

Having successfully solved the mystery of "The Adventure of the Blue Carbuncle" and, in the spirit of "the season of forgiveness," given the culprit his freedom, Sherlock Holmes and Dr. Watson prepared to enjoy their much-postponed evening meal.[1] The bird was not goose but rather Holmes's favourite, woodcock.

Whether or not Holmes and the Watsons had goose for Christmas dinner that year the world will never know. It is certain that, whatever the December 25th menus were for Holmes and his companion, the two did not dine together, for the second morning after Christmas was Watson's first opportunity to offer his friend "the compliments of the season." The failure of the Watsons to include Sherlock Holmes at their Christmas table may be looked upon by some as evidence that the Great Detective and Mrs. Watson were not on the best of terms, but that is not likely. The more plausible view of the facts is that the proffered Christmas invitation was courteously declined by Sherlock, who "loathed every form of society with his whole Bohemian soul,"[2] and who chose to remain at Baker Street with his work. Occasionally the Watsons "persuaded him to forego his Bohemian habits so far as to come and visit,"[3] but not on that particular Yuletide.

The meal of woodcock over which Holmes and Watson belatedly exchanged Christmas greetings did not suffer from the delay. The cooking time for woodcock is brief. We do not doubt that Mrs. Hudson waited until the two had returned to Baker Street before starting to cook the birds.

---

[1] Holmes had shown his preference for a hot clue over a hot dinner when he proposed: "I suggest that we turn our dinner into a supper and follow up this clue while it is still hot."

[2] "A Scandal in Bohemia."

[3] "The Adventure of the Engineer's Thumb."

A meal of woodcock is not easily re-created in mid-twentieth-century America. Availability deters most would-be diners, although the woodcock, or its close cousin, the snipe, is a native of the United States, and this delicacy is not unknown to hunters in the regions where the bird abounds.

The manner in which woodcock was prepared is offensive to most modern diners, to say nothing of most public health specialists. As in the case of all game birds, woodcock was typically eaten "high"—decomposition being taken for tenderness, and the flavour that we, in our age of refrigeration, call "rotten" having become an acquired taste. To further insult the modern palate, woodcock—as well as other small insect- and berry-eating birds—was properly cooked undrawn, that is, without removing the intestines. Indeed, many a gourmet considered the succulent entrails on toast to be the best part, and the meat of this sinewy bird only secondary. It was best cooked quickly before a brisk fire, with a piece of toast strategically placed to catch the precious "trail."

For those whose palates will allow them to enjoy the cooked intestines, a not over-aged woodcock may be prepared undrawn without becoming a health hazard. To accommodate these adventurers, or gourmets, as well as the more squeamish, we will offer two tasty versions of woodcock for the modern oven. The first is undrawn. The second is drawn, but stuffed with an acceptable substitute for the trail. Although the flavour of woodcock may not be simulated by other poultry, the drawn version may be prepared with substitutes. We suggest quail, squab, or Cornish hen in that order of preference, with the cooking times adjusted to the size of the bird.

> Carrot Soup
> Woodcock
> Brussels Sprouts
> Scalloped Potatoes
> Apple Pie

☞ Carrot Soup

Serves 6 to 8

    2 pounds fresh or frozen carrots
    4 ounces butter
    2 quarts beef or chicken stock
    1 to 2 teaspoons salt, or to taste
    A pinch of cayenne pepper

1) Pare and wash the carrots. Dice them or cut them into thin slices.
2) Melt 3 ounces of the butter in a stewpot.

3) Add the carrots and ½ cup of stock, and stew them, covered, in a 225°F. oven for 1 to 1½ hours. (Do not let them brown.)

4) Add the stock and simmer the soup until the carrots are soft (¾ to 1 hour).

5) Puree the soup in a blender.

6) Season it with salt and cayenne.

7) Boil it for 5 to 6 minutes, and skim it well.

8) Fold the remaining butter into the soup and serve it.

☞ A Classical Woodcock (Undrawn)

Serves 4

4 woodcock (8 ounces each)
2 teaspoons salt
½ teaspoon black pepper
4 slices bacon
1 ounce butter
2 tablespoons chopped shallots or onions
4 slices of bread
1 clove garlic
2 knife tips dried thyme
2 pinches cayenne pepper
2 teaspoons salt
2 tablespoons brandy
1 egg yolk
1 tablespoon grated Parmesan cheese
½ cup dry white wine
1 bunch watercress

1) Pluck the birds. Remove the windpipe, the eyes, and the spurs on the legs, but leave the intestines intact.

2) Singe the birds to remove the pinfeathers.

3) Rinse them thoroughly under cold water and dry them.

4) Bind the head and wings back and push the beak through the body and legs.

5) Season the birds with salt and pepper.

6) Roll a strip of bacon around the breast of each bird, and tie it securely with a string.

7) Heat the butter in a roasting pan; add the woodcock, and roast them

in a preheated 325° to 350°F. oven for 25 minutes. Turn them every 5 minutes.

8) Peel and chop the shallots or onions.

9) Toast the bread and remove the crusts.

10) Remove the woodcock from the oven.

11) Remove the bacon and chop it finely.

12) Heat the chopped bacon in a sauté pan. Add the shallots and garlic and sauté them for 5 minutes.

13) Remove the gizzards from the birds and discard them.

14) Remove the intestines. Chop them, and add them to the bacon-shallot mixture. Season it with thyme, cayenne pepper, and salt. Add the brandy and flame it.

15) Mix the egg yolk with half of the grated cheese and fold it into the intestine mixture.

16) Spread this mixture over the toast, sprinkle it with the rest of the cheese, and bake it under a broiler for 3 minutes.

17) Deglaze the drippings in the roasting pan with the white wine and reduce it by half (approximately 15 minutes).

18) Surround the woodcock with the pieces of toast and the watercress. Serve the sauce separately.

☞ A Semi-Classical Woodcock (Drawn)

Serves 4

4 woodcock (8 ounces each)
2 teaspoons salt
½ teaspoon black pepper, or to taste
8 ounces goose-liver *pâté*
½ teaspoon *Pâté* Spice (see recipe, p. 119)
2 truffles (optional)
4 slices of bacon
4 ounces butter
2 tablespoons chopped shallots or onions
4 slices of bread
2½ tablespoons brandy
1 cup heavy cream
½ bunch parsley

1) Pluck and draw the birds.

2) Singe them to remove the pinfeathers.

3) Rinse them thoroughly under cold water and dry them.

4) Bind the head and wings back, and push the beak through the body and legs.

5) Season the woodcock with salt and pepper.

6) Cut the liver *pâté* into ½-inch cubes and season it with *pâté* spice, salt, and black pepper. Dice the truffles and mix them well with the *pâté*.

7) Stuff the cavities with the *pâté* mixture.

8) Tie a strip of bacon around the breast of each bird.

9) Heat the butter in a roasting pan. Add the woodcock and roast them in a preheated 300° to 350°F. oven for 25 minutes, or until they are done, turning them every 10 minutes.

10) Remove the woodcock from the oven, take them from the pan and keep them warm.

11) Peel and chop the shallots or onions.

12) Toast the bread and remove the crusts.

13) Remove the bacon from the woodcock and chop it finely.

14) Heat the chopped bacon in a sauté pan. Add the shallots and sauté them for 5 minutes.

15) Remove the *pâté* stuffing from the woodcock and add it to the bacon-shallot mixture. Add ½ tablespoon of brandy and ignite it.

16) Spread this mixture over the toast.

17) Deglaze the roasting pan with 2 tablespoons of brandy, and ignite it. Remove it from the heat and add the heavy cream. Bring it to one boil. Remove it immediately from the heat and strain it. Taste it and adjust the seasoning.

18) Surround the woodcock with the toast pieces and garnish them with parsley. Serve the sauce separately.

☞ Scalloped Potatoes

Serves 4

>1 pound potatoes
>4 to 5 ounces butter, melted
>½ to 1 teaspoon salt, or to taste
>4 grinds of pepper
>⅓ cup stock

1) Peel the potatoes and cut them into ⅓-inch slices.

2) Butter a small square roasting pan, and cover the bottom of the pan with 1 layer of potatoes. Sprinkle with the melted butter, salt, and pepper. Repeat the process to make 3 layers of potatoes.

3) Pour the stock into the pan, and bake the potatoes in a preheated 300° to 325°F. oven for 45 minutes, or until they are tender and are browned on top.

☞ Brussels Sprouts

Serves 4

1 pound small Brussels sprouts
Water to cover the sprouts
½ to 1 teaspoon salt
4 ounces butter
3 to 4 tablespoons breadcrumbs
1 hard-cooked egg, chopped
1 teaspoon finely chopped parsley

1) Clean the Brussels sprouts, stem them, and cut them crosswise. Wash them well.

2) Cover them with slightly salted water and boil them until they are *al dente*.

3) Remove them from the heat and shock them with cold water.

4) Melt 3 ounces of butter and add the breadcrumbs. Brown them slightly. Add the chopped egg and parsley and mix well.

5) In a separate pan, heat the remaining 1 ounce of butter; add the sprouts and sauté them lightly. Top them with the breadcrumb mixture and serve.

☞ Apple Pie

Serves 6 to 8

The English Christmas pie is traditionally baked in an oval pie dish, symbolizing the Christ Child's cradle.

1¾ pounds fresh apples
Calvados or applejack to taste (optional)
Lemon juice
⅞ cup white sugar
⅓ cup brown sugar

3 tablespoons cornstarch
½ to 1 teaspoon cinnamon
A pinch of salt
4 ounces butter
2 cups flour

1) Peel and core the apples. Cut them into wedges.

2) Mix the apples, Calvados, lemon juice, ½ cup white sugar, ⅓ cup brown sugar, cornstarch, cinnamon (to taste), and salt together. Put the apple mixture into a buttered deep pie dish.

3) Mix the butter with the remaining sugar. Flake it into the flour. Add a pinch more salt and cinnamon. Mix together and sprinkle on top of the apple mixture.

4) Bake the pie in a 350° to 375°F. oven for 40 to 45 minutes.

☞

The Horrors of a
Country Inn

The Railway Arms

"I have unwittingly condemned you to the horrors of a country inn," apologized Holmes to Watson in "The Adventure of the Retired Colourman." And well he might apologize, for to Watson that particular night was not one of happy memories. He was stranded in an isolated English village, one of the nation's "most primitive," with Mr. Josiah Amberley, a sullen, miserly companion.

Holmes had sent Watson off on a wild goose chase. A false telegram, posted by some confederate of the Master's, had dispatched Watson with client Amberley to a remote vicarage at Little Purlington "in Essex . . . not far from Frinton." There they were to receive fresh information from a Vicar Elman. Upon arrival after a long, hot train ride, they were confronted with an outraged clergyman who knew nothing of the matter. Chuckled Holmes to Watson over the telephone, ". . . there is always Nature, Watson—Nature and Josiah Amberley—you can be in close commune with both." The faithful but temporarily ill-humoured Watson had been sent on the trip merely to assure that the old miser Amberley was away from London long enough to allow Holmes a free hand in the investigation.

We hasten to remind the reader that although Dr. Watson's journey was unpleasant in most respects, there need not be anything at all horrible about a country inn, which Holmes and Watson themselves were to prove on many occasions.

Doubtless Watson tried to enjoy his supper by ignoring his fellow traveller, who "grumbled at the expense of the journey . . . and was . . . clamourous in his objections to the hotel bill." We offer, here, a menu that is helpful to the effect:

Salt Herring Salad
Beefsteak and Kidney Pie
Glazed Turnips
Gooseberry Fool
Mushroom Toast

☞ Salt Herring Salad

Serves 4

½ cup diced salt herring
½ cup diced cooked beets
½ cup diced apples
Salt, if necessary
2 to 3 tablespoons white vinegar
⅓ teaspoon sugar
2 to 3 tablespoons oil

1) Soak the salt herring in cold water for 24 hours before using it in order to remove some of the salty flavour.
2) Combine all the diced ingredients and toss them well.
3) Taste and adjust the seasoning.
4) Add the vinegar, sugar and oil.
5) Allow the dish to rest for 30 minutes. Serve it with toast.

☞ Beefsteak and Kidney Pie

Serves 4 to 6

1½ pounds cubed sirloin or top round of beef
1 pound veal kidneys

1 to 1½ teaspoons salt
¼ teaspoon ground black pepper
Cooking oil
¼ cup flour
1 cup sliced mushrooms
¼ cup chopped onions
1½ cups water
½ tablespoon chopped fresh parsley
½ teaspoon Worcestershire sauce
Short Pastry (see recipe, page 84) or puff paste dough
1 egg mixed with 1 tablespoon milk

1) Trim the fat off the kidneys, peel off the skin, and cut them into 1-inch cubes.

2) Mix the cubed beef and the kidneys and season them with salt and pepper.

3) Heat a small amount of oil in a 14-inch skillet, and brown half of the meat at high heat. Repeat the same process with the remaining half.

4) Transfer all the meat to a heavy casserole. Add the flour to the meat and brown the flour over medium heat.

5) Add the mushrooms and the onions, stir the mixture well, and cook it a little longer. Add the water and mix it well to make a sauce. Season it with the parsley and the Worcestershire sauce.

6) Transfer the stew to a rectangular pan about 2 inches deep. Cover it with the dough; seal the edges well with an extra strip of dough. Brush it with the egg-and-milk mixture and pierce the dough with a fork. Decorate the top of the dough with any leftover pieces.

7) Bake it for 30 to 40 minutes in a 350°F. oven until the crust is golden brown.

☞ **Glazed Turnips**

Serves 4

1 to 1½ pounds turnips
2 ounces butter
1 tablespoon sugar
½ teaspoon salt
1 teaspoon chopped parsley

1) Peel the turnips and cut them into thumb-thick wedges. Blanch them slightly in salted water until they are *al dente*.

2) Heat the butter; add the sugar and heat it until it caramelizes.

3) Add the turnips and heat them slowly. Season them with salt. Garnish them with the 1 teaspoon chopped parsley.

☞ Gooseberry Fool[1]

Serves 4

    1 pint gooseberries
    1 to 2 ounces butter
    ½ cup sugar
    1 cup heavy cream

1) Put green gooseberries into a fireproof container or casserole and cover them tightly. Bake them in a moderate 350°F. oven until they are soft and well pulped.

2) While the berries are still hot, stir in the butter and sugar. Allow them to cool.

3) Puree them in an electric blender.

4) Whip the heavy cream. Fold the berry pulp into it. It is important that the two mixtures are of approximately the same consistency.

5) Chill it and serve it cold in individual glasses.

Note: Canned gooseberries may be used. Drain them before heating and pureeing them. Because canned berries are already cooked, they need not be baked, but only heated slightly. Other "fruit fools" may be made. For example, stewed apricots, cooked rhubarb, or fresh raspberries may be used in the same manner as canned gooseberries.

☞ Mushroom Toast

Serves 4

    24 medium-sized button mushrooms
    Parsley Butter (see recipe below)
    4 slices of toast

---

[1] Who felt more the fool, Watson or Amberley, when at the conclusion of the adventure they learned that the trip to Little Purlington had been only a ruse?

1) Separate the tops from the stems of the mushrooms. Use the tops only; reserve the stems for other uses.

2) Fill the cavities of the mushroom tops halfway with parsley butter, and bake them in a 350° to 400° oven for 5 to 10 minutes.

3) Set 6 mushrooms on each piece of toast, and put them under the broiler about 12 inches away from the source of heat for 2 to 3 minutes. Trim the crusts and serve the toast immediately.

PARSLEY BUTTER[2]

> 2 ounces butter
> 2 tablespoons chopped parsley
> 1 teaspoon lemon juice
> A pinch of white pepper

Mix the butter and parsley. Cream them together until they are smooth. Season with lemon juice and white pepper.

Note: This butter can be made in larger quantities and stored in the refrigerator. It is particularly decorative when still cold.

An Unnamed Hotel in Wallington

"Drive us to some decent hotel, cabby, where we may have some lunch."

No repast better illustrates Holmes's habit of suspending the unpleasantries of the moment while he enjoyed his food than the luncheon he shared with Dr. Watson at a hotel in Wallington during "The Adventure of the

---

[2] Recall how Sherlock Holmes uncovered "the dreadful business of the Abernetty family . . . by the depth which the parsley had sunk into the butter upon a hot day." ("The Adventure of the Six Napoleons.")

Cardboard Box." As Watson told it: "We had a pleasant meal together, during which Holmes would talk about nothing but violins, narrating with great exultation how he had purchased his own Stradivarius . . . this led him to Paganini, and we sat for an hour over a bottle of claret while he told me anecdote after anecdote of that extraordinary man." After this pleasant hiatus, the investigation proceeded: namely, to discover who had sent an elderly spinster, Miss Susan Cushing, two severed human ears, neatly packaged in coarse salt. Sherlock Holmes already knew the answer, and after his lunch, he and Dr. Watson went to the police station, where he put Inspector Lestrade on the trail of the criminal.

Cock-a-Leekie Soup
Roast Beef and Yorkshire Pudding
Marinated Cucumbers
Burnt Cream

☞ Cock-a-Leekie Soup[1]

Serves 4 to 8

4 cups clear chicken stock
1 eight-ounce leek, well washed and cut into *julienne* strips
8 ounces prunes (or 5 ounces pitted prunes)
½ cup diced chicken
1 to 2 pinches white pepper
½ to 1 teaspoon salt

1) Cook the *julienne* strips of leek in the chicken stock for approximately 15 minutes or until tender.

2) Cut the prunes in half and remove the stones. Add the prunes and the chicken meat to the soup, and bring it to a boil. Reduce the heat and

---

[1] Inspector Lestrade was with Holmes and Watson on this case, as he was in over a dozen of the adventures. The career of this dedicated detective, whom Holmes described as the "best of the professionals" (*The Hound of the Baskervilles*), spanned about forty years. No retirement after twenty years for Inspector Lestrade! We have not been able to solve the mystery of how he could be referred to as "rat-faced" in one adventure (*A Study in Scarlet*) and having "bull-dog features" in another ("The Adventure of the Second Stain"). In two adventures (*A Study in Scarlet* and "The Boscombe Valley Mystery") Lestrade was "lean and ferret like." In addition to these varied animal comparisons, his premature "cock-a-doodle" (not cock-a-leekie) of victory in "The Adventure of the Norwood Builder" links him with chicken.

simmer it slowly for 5 to 6 minutes. Season it to taste with white pepper and salt.

3) Remove it from the stove. Skim the top and serve it.

Note: Fine noodles may be added with the chicken and prunes.

☞ Roast Beef

Serves 12

6-pound rib roast

1) Preheat the oven to 450°F. Place the beef, fat side up, in a large, shallow roasting pan.

2) Roast the beef in the middle of the oven for 15 minutes. Then reduce the heat to 325°F. and continue to roast it, without basting, for about 1 to 1½ hours, or until the beef is done to taste.

With a meat thermometer, use the following guide:

> Rare—130°-140°
> Medium—140°-160°
> Well-done—160°-170°

Without a meat thermometer, use the following guide, beginning the roasting time after the oven has been turned down to 325°:

> Rare—approximately 20 minutes per pound
> Medium—approximately 25 minutes per pound
> Well-done—approximately 30 minutes per pound

This roast beef will serve 12. The English custom was to roast a large joint, with the intention of eating the leftovers the rest of the week.

☞ Yorkshire Pudding

Serves 6 to 8

2 eggs
½ teaspoon coarse salt
1 cup all-purpose flour

1 cup milk
¼ pound ground beef suet (optional)
2 tablespoons roast drippings or pork lard

1) Combine the eggs, salt, flour, and milk in a blender. Blend it at a high speed for 2 to 3 seconds. Turn off the machine. Scrape down the sides of the container, and blend again for 40 seconds. At this point ¼ pound of beef suet may be added to the above mixture.

2) Allow the mixture to rest for 1 hour at room temperature.

3) Preheat the oven to 400°.

4) Heat the fat in a 10 by 15 by 2½-inch roasting pan or in a muffin pan until it sputters.

5) Beat the batter again briefly and pour it into the pan or muffin pan. Bake it for 15 minutes at 400°F. Reduce the heat to 375°F. and bake it for 15 minutes more, or until the pudding has risen over the top of the pan and is crisp and brown. Serve it immediately.

Note: This recipe can be cut in half if fewer than 6 to 8 portions are desired.

By the addition of cooked sausages or any other cooked meat to the batter before it is baked, the Yorkshire pudding is transformed into another English favourite called "Toad in the Hole."

☞ Marinated Cucumbers

Serves 6 to 8

3 cucumbers (10 to 12 ounces)
¼ cup mayonnaise
¼ cup sour cream
⅓ cup or more plain white vinegar
1 tablespoon chopped dill
½ to 1 teaspoon salt, or to taste
2 to 3 grinds black pepper
½ medium-sized onion, sliced

1) Peel and slice the cucumbers.

2) Combine the mayonnaise, sour cream, vinegar, dill, salt, and pepper. Mix with the sliced cucumbers and onion.

3) Marinate overnight.

☞ Burnt Cream

Serves 6 to 8

    2 cups milk
    2 cups heavy cream
    4 egg yolks
    3 whole eggs
    1¼ cups sugar
    1 teaspoon vanilla extract

1) Scald the milk and the cream in a saucepan.

2) Combine the whole eggs and the egg yolks in a mixing bowl. Add ¾ cup of sugar and beat for 4 to 5 minutes.

3) Pour the milk and cream into the egg mixture and stir well. Mix in the vanilla extract.

4) Strain the custard into a 1-quart soufflé dish.

5) Place the soufflé dish in a pan of water, and bake it for 40 to 45 minutes at 350°F.

6) Cool it to room temperature.

7) Meanwhile, prepare a dark caramel by heating the remaining sugar until it caramelizes. Pour it over the top of the custard cream. Refrigerate the burnt cream before serving it.

Note: It is also possible to prepare the caramel first. Pour it into a mould before the custard. After the custard is chilled, it may then be unmoulded and the caramel will be on top.

The Crown Inn

". . . from the window we could command a view of the avenue gate, and of the inhabited wing of Stoke Moran Manor House."

Early in April in the year 1883, during "The Adventure of the Speckled Band," Holmes and Watson were summoned to Surrey to keep one of the most chilling vigils ever to be recorded in their career. They were awakened early one morning by the visit of a distraught Helen Stoner, who, alarmed by her twin sister's mysterious death, feared a similar fate herself. To help her, they had to confront the sinister Dr. Grimesby Roylott, Miss Stoner's stepfather, a man of violent temper who had "hurled the local blacksmith over a parapet into a stream." He had other exotic ways which were also to be feared. For example, his stepdaughter recounted: "He has at this moment a cheetah and a baboon, which wander freely over his grounds." It was to this man's dark and feared home, the ancient Stoke Moran, that Holmes and Watson went to learn what danger overshadowed their terrified client.

At their destination, they "had no difficulty in engaging a bedroom and sitting-room at the Crown Inn," from which they could watch the mysterious manor house for their opportunity to gain entrance to it. Advised Holmes, ". . . we shall have horrors enough before the night is over; for goodness' sake let us have a quiet pipe and turn our minds for a few hours to something more cheerful." During these watchful hours we fancy that they shared a pleasant meal in their rented sitting room, from which they awaited one of the most thrilling nights of their partnership.

> Crabmeat Cakes with Curry Sauce
> Lancashire Hot Pot
> English Suet Dumplings
> Raisin Pound Cake with Butter

☞ Crabmeat Cakes Stoke Moran[1]

Serves 4

½ pound King crab or Maryland blue crabmeat
1 ounce butter
1 tablespoon finely minced onion
2 ounces mushrooms, finely chopped
1 teaspoon chopped parsley
3 eggs
1 tablespoon grated cheese (mild Cheddar preferred)
1 tablespoon heavy cream, buttermilk, or wine
2½ cups breadcrumbs
¼ to ½ teaspoon salt, or to taste

---

[1] The sinister estate, Stoke Moran, was "of grey lichen-blotched stone, with a high central portion and two curving wings like the claws of a crab."

⅓ teaspoon thyme
3 tablespoons milk
½ cup flour
Oil for frying

1) Chop the crabmeat finely.

2) Heat the butter and sauté the onions until they are transparent.

3) Add the mushrooms and sauté them for 2 to 3 minutes.

4) Add the crabmeat and cook for 4 minutes.

5) Remove from the fire. Add the parsley; the cream, buttermilk, or wine; 1 egg; and the cheese. Mix well.

6) Add as many breadcrumbs to the mixture as it will take to make a workable substance.

7) Season it with salt and thyme.

8) Chill it in the refrigerator.

9) After it is cool, mould the mixture into round cakes. Press a small hole in the top of each cake with your finger.

10) Freeze the crab cakes to make the breading easier.

11) Mix 2 eggs with the milk.

12) Dip each crab cake into the flour, then into the egg mixture, and finally into the breadcrumbs. Shake off the excess breadcrumbs.

13) Deep-fry the cakes.

14) When they have been fried, dry them on a paper towel, and fill the cavity of each with a little curry sauce.

☞ Curry Sauce[2]

Makes approximately 1 cup

1 tablespoon butter
1 tablespoon flour
1 cup broth
1 tablespoon chopped ham
2 to 3 mushrooms, chopped
1½ teaspoons curry, or less
½ teaspoon salt, or to taste
Juice and peel of ½ lemon
1 egg yolk

---

2 Of all the sauces that may be served with crab cakes, we have chosen curry because of Dr. Grimesby Roylott's many years in India.

1) Melt the butter and gradually stir in the flour to make a light roux.

2) Add the broth to the roux and whisk it smooth.

3) Add the ham and mushrooms and cook for 15 minutes.

4) Strain the sauce and add the curry, salt, lemon juice, and lemon peel.

5) Bring it to a boil, remove it from the fire, and thicken it with the egg yolk.

Serve the sauce with the crab cakes. It is also excellent with lamb, chicken, and veal.

☞ Lancashire Hot Pot[3]

Serves 4

2-pound mutton shoulder, cubed
1½ ounces lard
1 cup diced onion
1 stalk leek, sliced (white part only)
⅓ cup tomato puree
3 to 4 tablespoons flour
½ to 1 teaspoon coarse salt, or to taste
½ teaspoon black peppercorns, crushed
⅓ teaspoon thyme
1 small bay leaf
Water to cover meat
¾ cup carrots, cut into large dice
2 ribs celery, cut into large dice
1 cup turnips, cut into large dice
4 small potatoes
1 tablespoon chopped parsley

1) Heat the lard and brown the meat in a heavy casserole. Add the onions, leek, and tomato puree. Sprinkle with flour.

2) Add the spices and water barely to cover. Simmer for about 45 minutes.

3) Meanwhile, blanch the vegetables and add them to the meat after the 45 minutes. Continue cooking them until the meat and vegetables are done and the potatoes are evenly cooked (approximately 20 to 25 minutes).

4) Sprinkle with chopped parsley.

---

[3] Lancashire hot pot was known all over England, and it was therefore not unusual that Holmes and Watson should eat it in Surrey.

☞ English Suet Dumplings

Makes 12 dumplings

2 ounces fresh beef suet, finely chopped
¼ cup finely chopped cooked smoked ham (⅛ pound)
2 cups fresh soft breadcrumbs (made from white bread, crushed in
   a blender)
2 teaspoons finely chopped parsley
1 teaspoon finely grated lemon peel
¼ teaspoon ground thyme
¼ teaspoon ground sage
½ teaspoon salt
Freshly ground black pepper
1 egg, lightly beaten
2 tablespoons butter
2 tablespoons oil

1) Combine the suet, ham, breadcrumbs, parsley, lemon peel, thyme, sage, salt, and pepper. Stir well.

2) Add the egg, and mix until the mixture can be gathered into a ball.

3) Divide it into 12 equal pieces and, with a moistened hand, shape each piece into a ball.

4) Melt the butter and oil over moderate heat in a 10- to 12-inch skillet. When it foams, drop in the balls. Cook them for 5 minutes or until they are golden brown, turning them frequently with a spoon.

5) Remove them from the fat and dry them on a paper towel. Serve them right away.

☞ Raisin Pound Cake

Make the pound cake described on p. 154, adding 1 cup of raisins to the dough before baking.

The Black Swan

". . . an inn of repute in High Street at no distance from the Station."

Sherlock Holmes was sympathetic to the plight of any distraught woman, whether her anguish came from a disappointed *affaire de coeur*, as for example that of Mary Sutherland in "A Case of Identity," or from mortal terror, as that of Helen Stoner in "The Adventure of the Speckled Band." Accordingly, when in "The Adventure of the Copper Beeches" Miss Violet Hunter wished to consult Holmes as to whether she should accept a certain position as governess, Holmes complained: ". . . my own little practice . . . seems to be degenerating into an agency for recovering lost lead pencils and giving advice to young ladies from boarding-schools." But he did not refuse her. Besides, as he confided to Dr. Watson, "It may turn out to be of more interest than you think." His hopes were not disappointed, for the case was to uncover motives of the most sinister sort in the offer of employment tendered to Miss Hunter.

Watson, however, was soon to raise hopes of his own which were later dashed. Having himself recently fallen in love with Mary Morstan,[1] he hoped that his companion would likewise succumb to the softer passions. Watson observed that Miss Hunter "was plainly but neatly dressed, with a bright, quick face, freckled like a plover's egg, and with the brisk manner of a woman who has had her own way to make in the world." She was the sort of woman who might be expected to appeal to the Master, and Watson noted "that Holmes was favourably impressed by the manner and speech of his new client." But Watson's hopes were to remain unfulfilled. Regretfully, Watson wrote at the conclusion of the story, "My friend Holmes, rather to my disappointment, manifested no further in-

---

[1] This inference is based on the chronology of William S. Baring-Gould (see *The Annotated Sherlock Holmes,* New York: Clarkson N. Potter, 1967, Vol. 2, p. 114), who places "The Adventure of the Copper Beeches" between Doctor Watson's engagement to Miss Mary Morstan in *The Sign of Four* and his marriage.

terest in her when once she had ceased to be the centre of one of his problems."[2]

Holmes made one of his rare exceptions to his rule of not mixing sleuthing and dining, when he and Watson joined Violet Hunter for lunch at the Black Swan Inn.[3] "She had engaged a sitting-room, and our lunch awaited us upon the table." There she recounted the most recent of the dark happenings at her place of employment, "The Copper Beeches." Before lunch Holmes had "devised seven separate explanations, each of which would cover the facts." By the end of the day, he had eliminated the six incorrect ones. Justice was restored.

The memory of the food may have grown cold in comparison with the stirring tale unfolded by Miss Hunter, but we have no doubt that it was tasty and tempting:

> Stuffed Turmeric Eggs
> Chicken Pie
> Dandelion Salad
> Chocolate Cream Nectar

☞ Stuffed Turmeric Eggs

Makes 20 egg halves

1½ teaspoons dry mustard
1½ teaspoons cornstarch
2   cups water
2   cups distilled white vinegar
1½ to 2 teaspoons sugar
½   teaspoon turmeric
10 hard-cooked eggs

1) Dilute the dry mustard and cornstarch with the water. Add the vinegar and spices. Boil for 2 minutes and allow to cool to room temperature.

---

[2] We are of the opinion that Sherlock Holmes carefully avoided any possibility of romantic entanglement during his detective career, but that he quite willingly succumbed after his retirement. (See p. 127.)

[3] This is one of the few inns identified with its correct name. Mr. William S. Baring-Gould has noted that it was highly recommended in Baedeker's *Guide to Britain* of 1897. (*The Annotated Sherlock Holmes*, New York: Clarkson N. Potter, 1967. Vol. 2, p. 122.) It maintained its good reputation through subsequent editions of Baedeker's as well, but, alas, it no longer graces the streets of Winchester.

2) Add the hard-cooked eggs to the liquid, and refrigerate them for 24 hours.

To Stuff the Eggs:

>   2 tablespoons oil or 2 to 3 tablespoons mayonnaise
>   1 tablespoon vinegar
>   ½ teaspoon mustard
>   Salt to taste
>   Chopped chives

1) Cut the eggs in half lengthwise.

2) Remove the egg yolks.

3) Wash the egg-white halves in slightly salted water, and dry them upside down on a paper towel.

4) Puree the egg yolk in a blender or a food mill, and whip it together with the other ingredients.

5) Pipe the stuffing into the egg-white cavities.

☞ Chicken Pie—the English Way

Serves 4 to 8

>   A 2- to 3-pound chicken
>   1½ quarts boiling water
>   1 to 1½ teaspoons salt
>   1 to 1½ teaspoons sugar
>   1½ cups cubed raw potatoes
>   1½ cups sliced onions
>   ¼ cup minced celery
>   ½ cup finely diced carrots
>   3 tablespoons butter or chicken fat
>   3 tablespoons flour
>   3 cups chicken stock
>   Pie crust or Biscuit Crust (see next page)

1) Wash the chicken well and dry it. Cut it into small pieces.

2) Place the pieces in a pot and cover them with 1½ quarts of boiling water. Add the salt and the sugar.

3) Cook the chicken covered in a hot oven (375° to 400°F.) until it is tender (approximately ½ hour).

4) Remove the chicken meat from the bones and place it in alternating layers with the vegetables in a shallow casserole.

5) Melt the butter, stir in the flour, and gradually add the chicken stock.

6) Pour it over the chicken pie mixture. Top it with pie crust or a biscuit crust and bake 45 to 60 minutes at 375°F., covering it with aluminum foil for the first 35 minutes so that the crust will not brown too rapidly.

BISCUIT CRUST

  2 cups all-purpose flour
  ½ teaspoon salt
  4 teaspoons baking powder
  6 tablespoons shortening
  ¾ cup milk

1) Sift the dry ingredients together and work in 3 tablespoons of shortening with the back edge of a spoon.

2) Moisten the dough with the milk, turn it onto a lightly floured board, and roll it to a ¼-inch thickness.

3) Spread half of the remaining shortening on the dough to within ½ inch of the edge. Fold the dough over and roll it out.

4) Repeat this process once more, using the remaining shortening.

5) Roll the dough to a thickness of ¾ inch.

6) Shape the dough into individual biscuits, using a small biscuit cutter. Place them on top of the chicken pie so that they almost touch each other.

☞ **Dandelion Salad**

Serves 4 to 8

  ½ cup white vinegar
  ½ tablespoon salt
  ⅓ tablespoon dry mustard
  ½ teaspoon sugar
  ⅓ teaspoon white pepper
  1½ cups salad oil
  Fresh young dandelion leaves

Combine the vinegar and seasonings. Mix them well. Taste and correct the seasoning if necessary or dilute with water. Add the oil and mix well again. Dip the dandelion leaves into the dressing and arrange them in a salad bowl. Grated onions or a small amount of garlic may be added to this recipe.

☞ **Chocolate Cream Nectar**

Serves 4

    2 one-ounce squares bitter chocolate
    1 cup strong coffee
    1 cup granulated sugar
    2½ cups water
    1 teaspoon vanilla extract
    4 tablespoons whipped cream

1) Melt the chocolate in a dry pan over low heat.
2) Add the coffee and simmer it for 2 minutes, stirring constantly.
3) Add the sugar and the water, and simmer for 5 minutes more.
4) Chill thoroughly.
5) Add the vanilla and pour into 4 glasses, each containing a tablespoon of whipped cream.

The Fighting Cock

". . . we approached the forbidding and squalid inn, with the sign of a game-cock above the door."

Of all the inns at which Holmes and Watson are known to have dined, the Fighting Cock, in the north of England, was by far the least promising. Our two friends approached this "forbidding and squalid inn" during "The Adventure of the Priory School," having followed a trail of clues across the moor. The clues were to the solution of a dastardly murder, and they led to the door of the Fighting Cock Inn. Reuben Hayes, the innkeeper, "far from gracious," indeed hostile, accepted their presence with the utmost reluctance.

Sherlock Holmes was not to be deterred—either in gaining the information that he needed or in enjoying his evening meal. Even under the most adverse circumstances, Holmes and Watson relaxed over their food. As Watson recounted this adventure, "It was nearly nightfall, and we had eaten nothing since early morning,[1] so that we spent some time over our meal." We fancy that the food was better than the squalid atmosphere of the place would suggest. Even a hungry Holmes would not tarry long over an unappetizing platter. His taste was too refined for that. Food was to be either enjoyed or left alone. We may, therefore, infer that a good meal was in store.

In a small country inn, the food was usually the responsibility of the innkeeper's wife. Although Holmes and Watson never met her (they "were left alone in the stone-flagged kitchen"), they were told of her reputation: "A kindly woman, but entirely under the control of her brutal husband." The meal was of the sort that could be prepared earlier in the day and kept warm until diners arrived. One such dish is jugged hare, and, when good, it is worth a detour to whatever inn serves it. We might note in passing that Holmes and Watson were able to find more than a good meal under the sign of the game-cock, for the sought-after clues were there as well.

Jugged Hare
French Bread
Cinnamon Apples

☞ **Jugged Hare[2]**

Serves 8

   3 cups red wine
   2 tablespoons oil
   1 large onion, cut into ⅛-inch slices

---

[1] So far as we know, all they had in the early morning was cocoa.

[2] This dish proved to be prophetic, because, before the adventure was over, Reuben Hayes was himself to be jugged—unlike the rogue Ryder, the "shrimp" of "The Adventure of the Blue Carbuncle," who ran like a scared rabbit when Holmes gave him his freedom. Rabbits were cooked in "The Adventure of the Norwood Builder" in Jonas Oldacre's woodpile, but were too charred to be edible. They were, indeed, too charred to be recognized. They might have been dogs, but Holmes suggested that Watson record rabbits.

3 to 4 whole juniper berries, crushed
1 large bay leaf
½ teaspoon dried rosemary
2 to 2½ teaspoons coarse (Kosher) salt
Freshly ground pepper to taste
1 5- to 6-pound hare (fresh or frozen)
1 pine branch
2 tablespoons flour
6 slices bacon, coarsely chopped
¼ cup finely chopped shallots
½ cup coarsely chopped celery
6 small carrots, coarsely chopped
3 tablespoons red currant jelly (or hare blood)
1½ cups stock
1 teaspoon dried thyme
2 teaspoons finely chopped parsley
2 small bay leaves

1) Combine the wine, oil, onion, juniper berries, bay leaf, rosemary, ½ teaspoon salt, and black pepper in a large bowl.

2) Rinse the hare well and dry it with a paper towel.

3) Cut the hare into 2-inch-square pieces and put it in the above marinade.

4) Make sure to turn the hare so that it will be covered with the marinade. Put the pine branch on top, and let it rest for 6 hours (or overnight) in the refrigerator. Turn the pieces occasionally. Remove the pine branch.

5) Drain the hare in a colander and set it into a bowl.

6) Reserve the liquid, but discard the onions and herbs.

7) Pat the pieces of hare with paper until they are dry. Coat them with flour, shaking each piece to remove the excess.

8) Cook the bacon in a 4- to 5-quart pot or casserole, over moderate heat, until it is crisp and brown. With a slotted spoon, transfer the bacon to a paper towel to drain it.

9) Add the hare to the fat remaining in the casserole and brown it evenly on all sides. Transfer the hare to a plate.

10) Pour off all but 2 tablespoons of fat; add the shallots, celery, and carrots, and cook for 5 to 8 minutes or until the vegetables are soft but not brown. Add the red currant jelly and mix well.

11) Pour in the marinade that has been reserved and the stock and bring to a boil, scraping any brown material clinging to the bottom and sides of the casserole.

12) Add the thyme, parsley, bay leaves, ½ teaspoon salt, and some ground pepper.

13) Return the hare and bacon to the casserole, cover it tightly and braise it in a hot oven for 40 to 50 minutes, or until the hare is tender. Adjust the seasoning.

☞ **French Bread**[3]

4 loaves

    2 ounces fresh compressed yeast
    2 tablespoons sugar
    ⅓ cup milk
   11 cups flour
    3 cups water
    2 tablespoons salt
    1 egg white
    1 ounce shortening
    Cornmeal to dust the pan
    4 tablespoons cornstarch
    2 cups boiling water

1) Cream the yeast and the sugar together, and add the milk, which has been warmed to body temperature.

2) Combine the flour, water, salt, egg white, and shortening in a bowl. Add the yeast mixture and knead the dough by hand for 25 to 30 minutes. If the dough mixture is too soft, up to 1 cup of additional flour may be added. (The dough might also be mixed with an electric mixer on medium speed for 12 to 15 minutes.)

3) Form the dough into cigar-shaped loaves. Make a lengthwise cut in the top of each loaf, and set them on a baking tray which has been dusted with cornmeal.

4) Cover the loaves with a dampened cloth and set them in a warm place to rise for 30 minutes, or until they have increased by ¾ of their original size.

5) Dilute the 4 tablespoons of cornstarch with a little water, and add it to 2 cups of boiling water.

6) Brush the loaves with the cornstarch mixture and bake them in a 400° oven until they are uniformly brown.

---

[3] With the breadcrumbs, Holmes demonstrated the peculiar pattern of cattle tracks that they had seen on their tramp across the moor. The hoofprints, he showed, made a pattern that could not be made by cattle, but only by a horse.

☞ Cinnamon Apples

Serves 8

2 pounds apples
3 ounces butter
6 tablespoons white wine
¾ cup sugar
3 teaspoons powdered cinnamon

1) Peel, quarter, and core the apples.

2) Heat the butter and add the apple wedges. Add the wine and braise them, covered, for 10 minutes, turning them a few times.

3) Mix the sugar and cinnamon together. Add it to the apples and cook them for 2 more minutes. Serve them warm in a glass bowl.

The Green Dragon

"A short drive took us to an old-fashioned tavern, where a sporting host . . . entered eagerly into our plans for the extirpation of the fish of the neighborhood."

In "The Adventure of Shoscombe Old Place," the role of the inn as a valuable repository of information comes into play. On a previous occasion, Holmes had advised Watson that the best place to go was "the nearest public-house. That is the centre of country gossip."[1] Accordingly, when Holmes was called upon to investigate some mysterious happenings at Shoscombe Old Place in Berkshire, he and Watson made straight for the Green Dragon at Crendall. There they posed as fishermen "who badly need some good Berkshire air." They contrived, as Watson reported, to "have our host in for a glass of his own wine and hold some high converse on eels and dace, which seems to be the straight road to his affections."

---

[1] That was Holmes's advice to Watson in "The Adventure of the Solitary Cyclist," after Watson had taken his inquiries to a London house agent instead.

We doubt that they could have discussed these aquatic creatures for long without touching upon the means by which they may be cooked, once they have been extracted from the water. We presume that the following recipes were mentioned that night:[2]

Fricassee of Eel

Dace with Beer

☞ Fricassee of Eel

Eel was much more highly regarded as a food in Holmes's day than it is in ours.

Serves 4

2 pounds fresh eel (not too thick)
4 ounces mushrooms
1 tablespoon butter
Juice of ½ lemon
1 chopped onion
2 scant tablespoons flour
Approximately 4 cups water
1 herb bunch (carrot, celery, leek, parsley)
1 to 1½ teaspoons salt, or to taste
⅛ teaspoon pepper, or to taste
2 to 3 tablespoons heavy cream
1 egg yolk
1 tablespoon chopped parsley, or to taste

1) Wash the mushrooms and cut them into large pieces. Sauté them in butter with a little of the lemon juice and some salt. Set them aside.

2) Sauté the chopped onion to a golden colour.

3) Add the fresh eel (cut into 1- to 2-inch lengths). Sauté it slightly.

4) Dust it with flour and cook for 2 to 3 minutes.

5) Add the water and mix it well with the flour.

6) Add the herb bunch, salt, and pepper. Simmer it for about 20 minutes.

7) Add the mushrooms and bring to a boil.

8) Mix the heavy cream with the egg yolk and fold into the sauce. Season with the rest of the lemon juice. Remove the herb bunch. Sprinkle the chopped parsley over the eel, and serve it with rice or noodles.

[2] See also Jellied Eel, p. 45.

☞ Dace with Beer

Serves 4

The dace is a swift, gregarious, little (up to 10 inches) freshwater fish. It may be cooked the same way as carp.

> 4 pounds dace (carp)
> 2 medium-sized onions
> 1 carrot
> 1 lemon
> 1 bay leaf
> 2 teaspoons salt
> ½ teaspoon pepper
> 1½ to 2 pints light beer
> 5 ounces gingerbread or gingersnaps
> 2 ounces butter

1) Cut the dace lengthwise in half or into thick pieces.

2) Dice the onions and carrot roughly and put them into a pot. Top the vegetables with the fish pieces.

3) Squeeze the lemon, reserving the juice. Separate the peel from the pulp, and drop the peel into the pot. Add the bay leaf, salt, and pepper.

4) Pour the beer over the fish and cover with a piece of buttered paper.

5) Bake in a 350° to 400°F. oven 25 to 30 minutes, or until the fish is done.

6) Remove the fish pieces from the pot and keep them warm.

7) Bind the fish broth with the grated gingerbread or gingersnaps. Boil for 2 minutes. Season with the lemon juice, fold in the butter, and strain over the dace.

8) Serve the fish with mashed potatoes and string beans.

Note: Carp, striped bass, bluefish, red snapper, or pompano would be suitable for this recipe. The cooking time would be reduced to 15 to 20 minutes in the case of striped bass and bluefish.

The investigation proceeded well, and by the following afternoon the strange mystery was almost solved. With some time to spare, they "did actually use our fishing tackle in the mill-stream, with the result that we had a dish of trout for our supper." To accompany the fresh fish, we offer the following:

> Cold Leek Soup
> Brook Trout Meunière

Potatoes O'Brian
Tossed Green Salad with Oil and Vinegar
Sherry Syllabub
Scotch Woodcock

☞ **Cold Leek Soup**

Serves 4 to 6

5 leeks, white part only
1 medium-sized onion, diced
3 tablespoons butter
6 medium-sized potatoes, peeled and diced
5 cups chicken broth
¼ to 1 tablespoon salt
2 cups heavy cream
2 tablespoons chopped fresh chives
2 to 3 tablespoons chervil (optional)

1) Chop the white of the leeks and sauté them and the onion in the butter. Do not brown them. They must remain white and limp.

2) Add the diced potatoes, the stock, and half of the salt. Cook for 40 minutes.

3) When the vegetables are done, strain the soup through a fine food mill or puree it in an electric blender.

4) Add the rest of the salt, the cream, and the chives. Mix well, and cool the soup. When it is cold, adjust the seasoning and serve it. If chervil is available, add 2 to 3 tablespoons of freshly chopped chervil leaves.

☞ **Brook Trout Meunière**[3]

Serves 4

4 trout
⅓ teaspoon salt, or to taste
Flour for coating the fish

[3] This recalls M. Oscar Meunier of Grenoble, who moulded the wax bust of Holmes that was used in "The Adventure of the Empty House."

6 tablespoons butter
4 lemon wedges
½ teaspoon chopped parsley

1) Rinse the trout carefully. Make an incision on both sides of each fish, approximately ⅛ inch deep. Season them slightly with salt and dip them in flour.

2) Sauté the fish in butter until they are golden brown on both sides.

3) Sprinkle them with lemon juice and chopped parsley.

4) Pour the brown butter over the trout. Serve them with a green salad.

☞ **Potatoes O'Brian**

Serves 4

1 pound potatoes
1 small green pepper
1 small red pepper
1½ ounces butter
½ ounce oil
½ teaspoon salt
⅛ teaspoon pepper

1) Wash, peel, and cut the potatoes into ½-inch dice. Dice the peppers to about the same size.

2) Heat the butter and oil and sauté the raw potatoes for about 20 minutes. After the first 10 minutes, add the peppers.

3) Season with salt and pepper and serve.

☞ **Tossed Green Salad with Oil and Vinegar**

Serves 4

2 cups water
1 cup vinegar
½ to 1 teaspoon salt, or to taste
½ teaspoon sugar
2 teaspoons chopped dill
½ cup oil
Greens

Mix together all the ingredients except the oil and the greens. Taste and adjust the seasoning. Add the oil. Dip the greens in the dressing, and arrange them on a plate or in a bowl.

☞ Sherry Syllabub

Serves 4

>   1 cup heavy cream
>   ½ cup sherry
>   Juice of ½ lemon
>   Grated rind of ½ lemon
>   2 tablespoons sugar

1) Whip the cream until it is stiff.
2) Fold in the other ingredients.
3) Chill before serving.

☞ Scotch Woodcock

Serves 4

>   2 English muffins, cut in half and toasted
>   4 medium-sized scrambled eggs
>   4 anchovy fillets
>   4 grinds black pepper, or to taste

Top each of the toasted muffin halves with the scrambled eggs and an anchovy fillet, and season each one with 1 grind black pepper.

The Westville Arms

"There's no other place, but I hear that it is clean and good."

The adventure known to the world as *The Valley of Fear* was no trifling matter. Holmes was alerted to a violent murder at the ancient

Sussex manor of Birlstone, almost simultaneously by two sources. The first news was in cipher from Porlock, a spy within the Moriarty organization. The second summons came from a visit by Scotland Yard's Inspector MacDonald. Although Sherlock Holmes was to travel no farther than Sussex, he was to uncover a tale of terror spanning two continents and reaching an unexpectedly tragic conclusion off the coast of a third.

Holmes's entrance into the case was the investigation of the reported death of Jack Douglas at his Birlstone residence, but the tale began years earlier in the Vermissa Valley of Pennsylvania, where the Pinkerton detective Birdy Edwards, alias McMurdo, alias Douglas, broke up a terrorist gang known as the Scowrers. The career of the brave "Douglas" closely paralleled that of the historical James McParlin, alias McKenna, who ended the reign of terror held by the Molly McGuires in Pennsylvania's eastern mining territory.

The Birlstone mystery was difficult to unravel. Everyone, even the Great Detective himself, was seemingly baffled, until one evening when Holmes returned to his room at the Westville Arms, ravenously hungry. Watson, who knew his friend's habits well, could tell from the excellent appetite that Holmes was nearing the solution of the mystery. Holmes assured Watson, "When I have exterminated that fourth egg, I shall be ready to put you in touch with the whole situation."

The repast that Holmes attacked with such revealing gusto was a "high tea," a meal not often mentioned in the Canon. "High tea," a late-nineteenth-century outgrowth of afternoon tea, had evolved into a sort of early supper, and for the less affluent, the entire evening meal. Mrs. Beeton[1] recommended the high tea as an excellent way for the ever increasing middle class to entertain graciously without a large staff. For Holmes, on this occasion, it was a nourishing prelude to his unveiling of the startling solution to the Birlstone mystery.

Stuffed Tea Eggs
Toast
Kidneys in Wine Sauce
Orange Cake

---

[1] The name Beeton is much beloved in the Sherlockian world, for it was through the publication of *A Study in Scarlet* in *Beeton's Christmas Annual* of 1887 that the world first knew the name of Sherlock Holmes. The Beeton of Gastronomy, Mrs. Isabella Mayson Beeton, was the wife of publisher Samuel O. Beeton. She was a recognized authority on Victorian cookery, having published her monumental *Book of Household Management* in 1861. The description of high tea is to be found in later editions of this work carried out by the editors of Ward, Lock & Co. after Mrs. Beeton's untimely death in 1865 at the age of 29 (*Mrs. Beeton's Everyday Cookery and Housekeeping Book*, 1890, p. 490, and *Mrs. Beeton's All About Cookery*, 1897, p. 404).

☞   **Stuffed Tea Eggs**

Makes 16 egg halves

8 eggs
Strong tea, brewed
Ginger
Fennel
Gin

1) Boil the eggs for 5 to 6 minutes.
2) Cool them and crack the shells without removing them.
3) Submerge the eggs in a strong tea solution, flavoured with the ginger, fennel, and gin. Marinate them for 24 hours. When the shell is removed, the egg will have a marbled appearance.

To Stuff the Eggs:
    2 tablespoons oil, or 2 to 3 tablespoons mayonnaise
    1 tablespoon vinegar
    ½ teaspoon mustard
    Salt to taste
    Chopped chives

1) Peel the eggs and cut them in half lengthwise.
2) Remove the egg yolks.
3) Wash the egg-white halves in slightly salted water and dry them upside down on a paper towel.
4) Puree the egg yolk in a blender or a food mill and whip it together with the other ingredients.
5) Pipe the stuffing into the egg-white cavities. Garnish the eggs with tomato slices, olives, anchovies, caviar, etc.

☞   **Kidneys in Wine Sauce**

Serves 4

    2 pounds kidneys[2]
    1 onion (3 ounces)
    1½ ounces margarine, or 4 tablespoons oil

[2] This recipe was originally written for veal kidneys, but lamb or pork kidneys will also serve the purpose nicely.

2 tablespoons flour
½ to 1 cup hot water
2 to 3 teaspoons salt, or to taste
⅓ teaspoon pepper, or to taste
2 tomatoes (total 10 ounces)
½ bunch parsley
2 tablespoons red wine

1) Cut the kidneys open lengthwise. Remove the skin, sinews, and fat.

2) Soak the kidneys for 60 minutes in cold water. Remove them and dry them with a towel.

3) Cut them into ½- to 1-inch thick strips.

4) Chop the onion coarsely.

5) Heat the margarine or oil. Sauté the onion for 5 minutes, or until transparent.

6) Add the kidneys; sauté them for a moment. Dust them with flour, and turn them until they are coated.

7) Add the water, salt, and pepper. Simmer them for 5 minutes.

8) Blanch the tomatoes. Remove the skins, cut them into quarters, remove the seeds, and dice them. Add them to the kidneys, and simmer them for 3 more minutes.

9) Finely chop the parsley, and add it together with the red wine to the kidneys. Serve them immediately.

☞ Orange Cake

Serves 10 to 12

2½ cups pastry or cake flour
1 tablespoon baking powder
½ teaspoon salt
½ cup butter
1½ cups superfine granulated sugar
2 tablespoons grated orange rind
1 cup orange juice
½ cup (4) egg whites

1) Sift the flour with the baking powder and salt and set it aside.

2) Cream the butter, gradually adding the sugar and beating it until it is light and fluffy. Add the orange rind and blend it in.

3) Add the flour mixture to the creamed mixture alternately with the orange juice, beginning and ending with the dry ingredients, and beating until it is smooth.

4) Beat the egg whites very stiff and fold them into the batter, folding them in just to the point that there are no remaining patches of white.

5) Pour the batter into two 8-inch round layer pans that have been buttered and floured. Bake them in a 350°F. oven for 25 minutes or until done.

6) Cool the pans for 5 minutes before turning the cake out onto a rack. Frost it with orange frosting.

ORANGE FROSTING

   2 large egg whites
   1 cup sugar
   ⅛ teaspoon cream of tartar
   ¼ cup orange juice
   1 tablespoon grated orange rind
   2 tablespoons light corn syrup

1) Combine all the ingredients in the top of a double boiler and blend them together.

2) Over boiling water, beat the mixture with an electric mixer until the frosting forms peaks when the mixer is lifted. Remove it from the heat, and continue beating until the frosting holds a definite shape and is cool.

The Chequers

"I think, Watson, that our lot . . . might lie in less pleasant places."

An inn, if good enough, was more than a mere convenience; it was also an incentive for Holmes to undertake an investigation away from London. During "The Adventure of the Creeping Man," the inn Chequers in

Camford was such a place, one "where the port used to be above mediocrity, and the linen was above reproach."

Camford was a university town, either Oxford or Cambridge, the precise identity having been deliberately obscured by Watson. Sherlock Holmes was called there to investigate the strange antics of Professor Presbury of that university. The location of the mystery inevitably raises an Oxford *vs.* Cambridge debate.

Holmes's familiarity with the inn Chequers might suggest that Camford, whichever of the two universities it was, was Holmes's own school. The Reverend Stephen Adams, however, who asserted that Holmes was from neither Oxford nor Cambridge but rather the University of London, has pointed out that familiarity with an inn means nothing.[1] A student will, quite likely, be familiar with all the local pubs, but not necessarily with the linen of the town's hotels. We must assume that Holmes's acquaintance with the Chequers came from a stay during some previous investigation.

The one recorded Holmesian sojourn at an inn of a specific university town was in Cambridge during "The Adventure of the Missing Three-Quarter." Was it there that the Master acquired his experience with this favoured hotel? Perhaps, but in the earlier adventure, Holmes referred to Cambridge as "this inhospitable town," whereas Camford was "this charming town." If Camford referred to Cambridge, we must presume that the different descriptions are the direct result of the varying circumstances under which Holmes visited the town. In the earlier adventure, those whom he met were none too cordial. On the latter occasion, his clients were on hand to welcome him (although we cannot say much for the hospitality of Professor Presbury, the object of the investigation).

On the other hand, Camford could just as well have been Oxford, and Holmes's earlier stay at the inn could have taken place during any one of the adventures that went unrecorded or unmentioned. Indeed, we cannot rule out "The Adventure of the Three Students" as the occasion during which Holmes had stayed at the Chequers. Although he and Watson were not staying at an inn when the story opened, they may have spent a night or two there while they were seeking their more long-term lodgings. Because the university of the "Three Students" is not identified, this, of course, does not help locate the Chequers.

It is unfortunate, then, that we cannot locate this fine inn, and learn whether through the years it has maintained its good reputation for port and linen. We may, however, have a drink, and toast the Master as we recall the time he and Watson were "seated in the sitting-room of the ancient hotel, with a bottle of the famous vintage of which Holmes had

[1] In "Holmes—Student of London?" *Sherlock Holmes Journal,* Winter, 1955, 2, pp. 17–18.

spoken on the table." To go with the port, the inn would doubtless have provided some sort of canapé. We offer the following suggestions:

> Chestnuts with Bacon
> Deep-fried Olives and Cheese
> Cubed Ham with Mustard-Orange Sauce
> Crumpets

☞ Chestnuts with Bacon

Serves 4

½ pound chestnuts
½ pound bacon

1) Wash the chestnuts and cut slightly into the shells with a knife.
2) Toast them in the oven.
3) Peel them and wrap each chestnut in a piece of bacon, and secure it with a toothpick.
4) Bake them in a 300° to 350°F. oven until the bacon is crisp.

Note: This recipe is excellent, as well, when made with water chestnuts.

☞ Deep-Fried Olives and Cheese

Serves 8

1 jar pitted olives
1 cup cubed cheese (Swiss, Camembert, or mild Cheddar)
½ cup flour
1 egg, beaten
1 cup breadcrumbs
Oil for deep-frying

1) Soak the olives in water for 24 hours and dry them well.
2) Dip the olives and the cheese cubes into the flour, then into the beaten egg, then into the breadcrumbs. Shake off the excess breadcrumbs.
3) Deep-fry them and serve them hot with toothpicks.

☞ Cubed Ham with Mustard-Orange Sauce

Serves 8

½ pound ham, cut into cubes
8 tablespoons orange marmalade
6 tablespoons hot mustard
4 tablespoons red wine
5 tablespoons chopped onions

1) Mix the marmalade, mustard, wine, and onions together well. Allow to rest for ½ hour.

2) Serve the ham cubes with the sauce.

And after Sherlock Holmes had discovered the reason for Professor Presbury's odd behaviour, he did not hasten away from Camford without another visit to this charming hotel: "There is an early train to town, Watson, but I think we shall just have time for a cup of tea at the Chequers before we catch it." Tea and crumpets would have been just perfect for this light repast, perhaps accompanied by a soft-boiled egg or topped with a poached egg.

☞ Crumpets

Makes 10 to 12

¾ ounce fresh compressed yeast
2 cups lukewarm milk
1 ounce butter
1 egg
1 pinch salt
3 to 4 cups flour

1) Mix the yeast with a little of the lukewarm milk.

2) Mix the rest of the milk with the butter and heat it to lukewarm.

3) Beat the egg, and add the egg, salt, and flour to the milk and butter. Mix well.

4) Add the yeast and mix well again.

5) Cover the dough and allow it to rest for 15 minutes.

6) Shape the dough into about 10 to 12 round balls and, if desired, mould each in a ring 3 to 4 inches in diameter. Allow them to rise for 15 to 20 minutes.

7) Bake them on a buttered tray in a 400°F. oven until they are light brown. They may be served fresh, or, after they are cold, split open and toasted. Serve them with butter.

Note: This recipe allows the crumpets to be baked in the oven. Traditionally, however, they are shaped in rings and baked on a griddle. This may be done with this recipe too. Empty tuna-fish cans with the tops and bottoms cut off make adequate rings.

The Hereford Arms

"The sofa is much superior to the usual country hotel abomination."

Mr. Sherlock Holmes's cases took him to all corners of England (to say nothing of the entire world), and so it was that "The Boscombe Valley Mystery" found Holmes and Watson "flying westward at fifty miles an hour" to investigate a murder, "instead of quietly digesting their breakfasts at home." At their destination, they stayed at the Hereford Arms in the country town of Ross. Beginning his investigation upon his arrival, Holmes had all but concluded the case by lunch the next day. At least he was able to furnish Inspector Lestrade with a description of the murderer: ". . . a tall man, left-handed, limps with the right leg, wears thick-soled shooting-boots and a gray cloak, smokes Indian cigars, uses a cigar-holder, and carries a blunt pen-knife in his pocket." Then, in the words of Watson's chronicle, "Having left Lestrade at his rooms we drove to our hotel, where we found lunch upon the table."

At lunch, Holmes appeared silent and thoughtful as he and Watson sat down to their meal. After "the cloth was cleared," Sherlock Holmes reviewed with Watson some of the perplexing features of the case. (Note that the typical behaviour—that of not discussing a case over a meal—held true here, too.) The silent meal and the pained expression on the Master's face, we soon learn, were from his contemplating the deeper aspects of the matter. No sooner had Holmes reviewed the facts with Watson than the murderer himself entered the room, having been summoned by Sherlock Holmes. The interview confirmed what Holmes had already inferred and added a few hitherto unknown details.

No one could dine in Herefordshire without enjoying the cider for which the region is famous—in moderation, of course, out of respect for its high alcohol content. The other items on the menu suggest themselves quite readily:

> Welsh Pickled Fruit
> Pickled Onions and Mushrooms
> Beet Eggs
> Ham in Crust
> Red Currant Flan
> Welsh Rarebit

☞ Welsh Pickled Fruit

Serves 10 to 12

5 large ripe tomatoes, peeled
3 peaches
3 pears
2 medium-sized white onions
1 large green pepper
1 cup white vinegar
1 tablespoon coarse salt
2½ cups white sugar
1 teaspoon pickling spices in cheesecloth

1) Quarter the tomatoes, peaches, and pears. Peel and slice the onions. Cut the green pepper in half, remove the seeds, and slice it thinly.

2) In a large saucepan, boil the vinegar, salt, and sugar. Add the pickling spices and all the other ingredients. Bring to a boil and simmer for about 1½ hours or until the mixture will jell slightly when cool.[1] Transfer it to a serving bowl, cool at room temperature, remove the cheesecloth packet of spices, and chill for several hours before serving.

---

[1] To test this, put a small amount into a saucer and place it in the refrigerator for a few minutes.

☞ Pickled Onions and Mushrooms

Makes 3 cups

    1 pound pearl onions
    1 pound fresh tiny mushrooms
    ½ cup salt
    3 cups malt vinegar
    ½ cup sugar
    3 cloves
    2 tablespoons mixed pickling spices

1) Pour boiling water over the pearl onions; allow them to stand for 5 minutes, then drain and cool under cold water. The onions can then be peeled easily.

2) Cut the stems off the mushrooms and wash them under cold water. Drain them.

3) Mix the onions and mushrooms and sprinkle them with the salt. Mix them well. Marinate them 5 to 6 hours under refrigeration.

4) Wash the onions and mushrooms under cold water and drain them well.

5) Combine the remaining ingredients and boil them until the sugar is dissolved. Add the onions and mushrooms and boil them briskly for 5 minutes.

6) Transfer the vegetables to a serving dish. Pour over enough liquid to cover them and chill them for several hours before serving.

This hors d'oeuvre may be prepared 2 to 3 days ahead.

☞ Beet Eggs

Makes 16 eggs

    16 hard-cooked eggs
    2 tablespoons whole allspice
    2 tablespoons whole peppercorns
    4 cups white vinegar
    2 cups beet juice (drained from cooked beets)
    1 to 2 teaspoons sugar

1) Shell the hard-cooked eggs. Put them in a stone crock or a plastic container.

2) Tie the allspice and peppercorns in a piece of cheesecloth.

3) Heat the vinegar, beet juice, spice bag, and sugar. Bring to a boil and simmer for 5 minutes.

4) Remove the spice bag. Pour the hot liquid over the eggs, covering them completely.

5) Allow the eggs to cool, then refrigerate them in the marinade for 24 hours.

☞ Ham in Crust

Serves 8

4 pounds ham
1½ tablespoons butter
1 tablespoon oil
1 diced turnip
1 diced carrot
1½ diced celery ribs
½ onion studded with 2 cloves
½ to 1 cup port wine
1 cup heavy cream
4 to 5 grinds pepper
⅓ teaspoon grated nutmeg
2 pounds of dough: Brioche dough (½ recipe, see p. 39), rye dough
   (1 recipe, see p. 104), or French bread dough (½ recipe, see
   p. 201)
1 egg yolk

1) Have the butcher remove the bone from the ham, or use a boneless ham.

2) Remove the skin and most of the fat from the ham.

3) Put the ham into a large casserole with the butter and oil and the vegetables. Cover the casserole and cook the ham over medium heat for 15 minutes.

4) Add the port wine, cover it again, and simmer for 30 minutes.

5) Add the heavy cream and simmer slowly for 1 hour, or until the ham is tender. Season it with pepper and nutmeg.

6) Remove the ham from the sauce and let it cool until the surface of the ham is just warm. Reserve the sauce.

7) Divide the brioche dough in half, and roll the halves out on a floured pastry board. Each half should be somewhat larger than the shape of the pan in which the ham will be baked.

8) Butter and flour the baking pan. Line it with half of the dough and

lay the ham on it. Spoon a little sauce over the ham. (The ham may be put in whole, or it may be pre-sliced, and reshaped after each slice has been coated with some sauce.)

9) Beat the egg yolk and brush the edges of the dough with it.

10) Cover the ham with the remaining dough and pinch the edges together to seal it tightly. Let the pan rest in a warm place for 30 minutes to allow the dough to rise. Brush the dough with the rest of the beaten egg yolk.

11) Bake the ham in a preheated 350° to 400°F. oven for 20 to 25 minutes. Serve it immediately. Serve the remaining sauce in a sauce boat.

☞ Red Currant Flan

Serves 8 to 12

3 eggs, separated
2 tablespoons cold water
1 cup sugar
3 drops vanilla extract
½ cup plus 1 tablespoon flour
½ cup plus 1 tablespoon cornstarch
1 teaspoon baking powder
Butter or margarine to grease the pie tin
1¾ pounds fresh red currants
¾ cup water
1 piece of lemon peel
3 tablespoons dry brown breadcrumbs (made from rolls) or cake crumbs
½ cup heavy cream
1½ ounces almonds

1) Whip the egg whites with 2 tablespoons of cold water until they are stiff (meringue).

2) Whip ⅔ cup sugar and the vanilla into the egg whites.

3) Fold the egg yolks into the mixture.

4) Mix the flour, cornstarch, and baking powder together and fold them slowly into the mixture.

5) Grease an 8- or 9-inch pie tin and fill it with the mixture.

6) Smooth the top with a spatula and bake it in a preheated oven for 45 minutes at 350° to 400°F.

7) While the cake is in the oven, remove the stems of the currants, wash them, and dry them. If canned berries are used, drain them.

8) Bring 5 tablespoons of sugar, ¾ cup water, and the lemon peel to a boil and simmer for 5 to 8 minutes. Add the berries and simmer them on low heat for 1 minute. *Do not boil, or the berries will crack open.*

9) Remove the berries from the syrup with a slotted spoon and set them aside.

10) Remove the cake bottom from the oven; cool it for ½ hour, then unmould it, and allow it to cool further.

11) Sprinkle bread or cake crumbs over the cake and top with the berries.

12) Reduce the syrup over medium heat for 15 to 20 minutes and pour it over the berries. Allow it to cool.

13) Whip the cream, add the remaining sugar, and pipe it as a border around the flan. Decorate the top with almonds.

Note: Blueberries may be used instead of currants, but they should be used raw, not heated in the syrup.

☞ Welsh Rarebit

Serves 8

1 pound Cheddar cheese
¼ cup beer
1 teaspoon mustard
A pinch of cayenne pepper
8 slices buttered toast

1) Melt the cheese with the beer in the top of a double boiler. Add the mustard and cayenne.

2) Pour over the buttered toast, and serve piping hot.

☞

Appendix

MENU NOTES

1. References to gustatory events, large and small, abound in the Canon. One irrepressible researcher has discovered 198 references to food or dining (J. B. Shaw, Alimentary, My Dear Watson, BSJ 17, No. 2, (June, 1967), pages 98-100).

   Accordingly, wide latitude exists in formulating an epicurean repast of true 1895 canonical dimensions. Fortunately, one need not resort to the type of meat that Silver Blaze, Shoscombe Prince, or the Baskerville Hound bring to mind. Nor, despite the existence of epicurean recipes for this type of rodent (Larousse Gastronomique, Crown Pub. New York (1961) p. 803) did we think it necessary to provide any offering associated with the Giant Rat of Sumatra. If indeed the world is ready for its introduction, this is neither the time nor the place. The same holds true for Sahara King (The Veiled Lodger), even though we are assured that "all recipes for beef are suitable for lion." (Larousse Gastronomique, p. 587). Other foods were eliminated on non-gastronomical grounds: an appetizer of orange pips would scarcely provide the auspicious beginning for which we strive; goose has not been included because a true canonical stuffing (i.e. a blue carbuncle in each crop) would prohibitively inflate the cost. Finally, we have rejected Ned Hunter's curried mutton, canonicity demanding that it be served up with "some powerful drug" (Silver Blaze).

   Hearty appetite, then, and may we look to the words of the Master: "There is cold partridge on the sideboard, and a bottle of Montrachet. Let us renew our energies before we make a fresh call upon them"

2. Oysters: "Shall the world, then, be overrun by oysters?" Holmes asks, in the Dying Detective. Better that it be overrun by oysters, we reply, than by the Moriartys, Morans, Sylviuses, VonGruners, and Milvertons. Probably, Athelney Jones would have agreed (The Sign of the Four).

3. Eggs: The Watsonian Chronicle, in fact, is overrun not by oysters, but by eggs. It was, no doubt, a staple of Mrs. Hudson's breakfast, and it was Holmes himself who said: "My dear Watson, when I have exterminated that fourth egg I will be ready to put you in touch with the whole situation." Sherlockians need not consume four eggs any more than they need devour six napoleons for dessert. See footnote 15, infra.

4. Prawn salad: There is no direct Bakerian evidence that Holmes ever ate shrimp. But its canonicity was settled when Holmes used that epithet to describe the rascal Ryder (The Blue Carbuncle).

5. Eel and Dace: See footnote 6, infra.

6. Trout: While working on the Shoscombe mystery, Holmes and Watson went fishing in the mill-stream "with the result that we had a dish of trout for our supper." At the time, the two were staying at the Green Dragon Inn, where they held "high converse upon eel and dace". The latter two foods are included here; green dragonmeat has been discreetly omitted.

7. Pate de foie gras pie: For a time, this delicacy was shrouded in mystery, prompting one critic (M. Rodell, BSJ (OS) 2, No. 1, Jan. 1947, 35-37) to declare that Watson invented it, when describing the "epicurean little cold supper" that marked the termination, in more ways than one, of the Noble Bachelor. But good Watson was libelled; the dish was authentic (Mrs. Ellet, The Practical Housekeeper; A Cyclopaedia of Domestic Economy, Stringer and Townsend, New York (1857), p. 412).

8. Tongue: See Footnote 14, infra.

9. Pheasant: Another food, offered to, but declined by, Lord Saint Simon, The Noble Bachelor. The words of the Great Detective, uttered in an entirely different context, are particularly appropriate: "If you will have the goodness to touch the bell, Doctor, we will begin another investigation, in which also a bird will be the chief feature." (The Blue Carbuncle).

10. Roast Beef: A cut off the old joint, no less, which, sandwiched between two rounds of bread, provided sustenance for Holmes, when starting on an expedition in The Beryl Coronet.

11. Duck: In The Gloria Scott, Holmes recounts his visit to Donnithorpe, at Old Trevor's estate, where he engaged in "wild duck shooting in the fens." While there is no specific mention of his eating the duck, he does proclaim himself "somewhat of a fowl fancier," in The Blue Carbuncle.

12. Pork: Not all pigs were made to suffer the indignities that befell the one swinging from a hook in the ceiling at Allardyce's back shop, (Black Peter). Others, we fancy, found their way to Victorian dining tables, reappearing as Gallantine of Pork. As for the Sauce Oxford, it is not our intention to rekindle the controversy pertaining to the college that Holmes attended, but we will not yield to those commentators who would have it Sauce Cambridge.

13. Green Peas: In The Three Students, the landlady, said Holmes, "babbled of green peas at seven-thirty." The parsley butter is added, as a reminder that the imperishable Holmes solved the dreadful Abernetty business, by determining how deep the parsley had sunk into the butter.

14. Peaches: Holmes, in the Hound, encountered tinned tongue and two tins of peaches.

15. Napoleon: No Sherlockian menu is complete without some reference to professor James Moriarty, "the .... of crime." It is not necessary, however, to eat six of them.

16. Tokay and Claret: Two of the Sacred wines. During the Adventure of the Cardboard Box, Holmes, drinking claret, regaled Watson with anecdotes of Paganini. The tokay brings forth a more ominous connection: that of the villain Von Bork, who, after being trapped by Holmes, was not allowed to enjoy the tokay from Franz Joseph's special cellar at the Schoenbrunn Palace.

17. The tea will be served with lemon, sugar, cream, or honey. The honey was flown here from a certain bee farm in Sussex.

Sherlock Holmes at the C.I.A.:
A Commemorative Dinner

In New York's mid-Hudson Valley, the initials C.I.A. connote not in-
trigue but good eating. High above the lordly Hudson River stands the
Culinary Institute of America, where some of the finest chefs in the
United States are trained. There, on June 2, 1973, more than a hundred
Sherlock Holmes enthusiasts gathered in the Great Hall for a feast commemorating the Great Detective of Baker Street and his faithful chronicler. On these pages are reproductions of the menu from this memorable
feast.

MENU [1]

Oysters Athelney Jones [2]

Variety of Eggs, Farçi [3]

Prawn Salad, Ryder [4]

Hyckory Wood Smoked Eel, Dace Shoscombe [5]

Trout Poché au Vin Blanc [6]

Pate de fois gras pie, St. Simon [7]

Baskerville Beef Tongue, Sauce Chantilly [8]

Noble Smoked Pheasant, Moulton [9]

Roast of Beef, English Style, Sauce Remoulade [10]

Donnithorpe Duck, from the fens [11]

Gallantine of Pork, Sauce Oxford [12]

Gilchrist Green Peas, Parsley Butter Abernetty [13]

Peaches Cartwright [14]

Napoleon a la Beppo [15]

Claret   Tokay [16]

Honey [17]

Beverages

S. H.

Bibliography

We have drawn upon many sources, both culinary and literary, for background and ideas for this work. Listed here are only those books and articles that are specifically cited in the preceding chapters.

ADAMS, STEPHEN. "Holmes—Student of London?" *Sherlock Holmes Journal*, Winter, 1955, 2, 17–18.

ASHER, RICHARD. "Holmes and the Fair Sex," *Sherlock Holmes Journal*, Summer, 1955, 2, 15–22.

BARING-GOULD, WILLIAM S. *Sherlock Holmes of Baker Street*, New York: Clarkson N. Potter, 1962.

BARING-GOULD, WILLIAM S., ed. *The Annotated Sherlock Holmes* (2 vols.), New York: Clarkson N. Potter, 1967.

BARNIKELL, DIETMAN. *A Biographical Sketch of Who Is Who on the Menu*, published serially by *The Culinarian*, the official publication of the Chefs' Association of the Pacific Coast. Privately circulated mimeograph.

BEETON, MRS. ISABELLA MARY MAYSON. *The Book of Household Management*, London: S. O. Beeton, 1861. Reproduced in facsimile by Jonathan Cape, Ltd., printed in the United States by Farrar, Straus and Giroux, 1969.

——. *Mrs. Beeton's All About Cookery*, London: Ward, Lock & Co., 1897.

——. *Mrs. Beeton's Everyday Cookery and Housekeeping Book*, London: Ward, Lock & Co., 1890.

BIGELOW, S. TUPPER. "Bar Tailed Geese," *Sherlock Holmes Journal*, Spring, 1964, 6, 108–109.

——. "Sherlock Holmes Was No Burglar," *Baker Street Journal Christmas Annual*, 1958, pp. 26–37.

BLAU, PETER. "In Memoriam: Muzaffer ad-Din," *Baker Street Journal*, 1974, 24, 141–145.

BRISTOWE, W. S. "The Three Students in Limelight, Electric Light, and Daylight," *Sherlock Holmes Journal*, Summer, 1956, 3, 2–5.

CHRIST, JAY FINLEY. "The Gasogene," *Baker Street Journal*, 1946, 1 (old series), 69.

DALTON, PATSY. "Canon Fodder," *Sherlock Holmes Journal*, Autumn, 1974, 11, 112–116.

DEWAAL, RONALD B. *The World Bibliography of Sherlock Holmes and Dr. Watson*, Boston: New York Graphic Society, 1974.

DOYLE, ARTHUR CONAN. *The Complete Sherlock Holmes,* Garden City: Doubleday.

EDITOR'S NOTE, *Sherlock Holmes Journal,* Spring, 1961, 5, 35–36.

ELLET, MRS. ELIZABETH FRIES. *The Practical Housekeeper: A Cyclopaedia of Domestic Economy,* New York: Stringer and Townsend, 1857.

HENCH, PHILLIP S. "Of Violence at Meiringen," in E. W. McDiarmid and Theodore C. Blegen, eds., *Exploring Sherlock Holmes,* LaCrosse: Sumac Press, 1957, pp. 97–120.

HILL, BENSON E. *Popular Cookery: or a Diary of Good Living,* London: A. Hall, Virtue & Co., 1842.

JOHNSON, SAMUEL. *Journey to the Western Islands of Scotland,* London: 1775.

KNOX, RONALD A. "Studies in the Literature of Sherlock Holmes," in James Holroyd, ed., *Seventeen Steps to 221B,* London: George Allen & Unwin, 1967, pp. 30–45.

McLAUCHLIN, RUSSELL. "Mrs. Hudson Speaks," *Baker Street Journal,* 1947, 2 (old series), 329–331.

McPHARLIN, PAUL. "221B—Certain Physical Details," *Baker Street Journal,* 1947, 2 (old series), 180–194.

MORLEY, CHRISTOPHER. "In Memoriam Sherlock Holmes," Introduction to Arthur Conan Doyle, *The Complete Sherlock Holmes,* Garden City: Doubleday.

MORROW, L. A. "More Letters from Somewhere," *Baker Street Journal,* 1968, *18,* 144–146.

OFFORD, LENORE GLEN. "The Brief Adventure of Mrs. Turner," *Baker Street Journal,* 1946, *1* (old series), 253–259.

PATTRICK, ROBERT R. "The Case of the Superfluous Landlady," *Baker Street Journal,* 1953, *3,* 241–243.

PEARSON, HESKETH. *Conan Doyle,* New York: Walker & Co., 1961.

PRATT, FLETCHER. "The Gastronomic Holmes," *Baker Street Journal,* 1952, 2 (new series), 94–99.

RODELL, MARIE. "Living on Baker Street," *Baker Street Journal,* 1947, 2 (old series), 35–37.

RORER, SARAH TYSON. *Mrs. Rorer's Philadelphia Cookbook,* Philadelphia: Arnold, 1886.

ROSENBERG, SAMUEL. *Naked Is the Best Disguise,* Indianapolis: Bobbs-Merrill, 1974.

ROSENBLATT, ALBERT. "On *Pâté de Fois Gras* Pie: In Defense of Watson," *Baker Street Journal,* 1973, *23,* 103.

ROSENBLATT, JULIA. "Who Was Tonga and Why Were They Saying Such Terrible Things About Him?" *Baker Street Journal,* 1975, *25,* 140–141.

ROSENBLUM, MORRIS. Letter to the Editor, *Baker Street Journal,* 1947, 2 (old series), 438–439.

SAYERS, DOROTHY. *Unpopular Opinions,* London: Victor Gollancz, 1946.

SHAW, JOHN BENNETT. "Alimentary, My Dear Watson," *Baker Street Journal,* 1967, *17,* 98–100.

SMITH, HENRY. *Classical Recipes of the World,* New York: Macmillan, 1955.

SONNENSCHMIDT, FREDERIC H., and NICOLAS, JEAN F. *The Professional Chef's Art of Garde Manger,* Boston: Cahners, 1973.

STARRETT, VINCENT. *The Private Life of Sherlock Holmes,* Chicago: University of Chicago Press, 1960.

WELLMAN, MANLY WADE. "The Great Man's Great Son," *Baker Street Journal,* 1946, *1* (old series), 326–336.

WHITE, FLORENCE. *Good Things in England,* London: Jonathan Cape, 1932.

ZEISLER, ERNEST BLOOMFIELD. "A Pigment of the Imagination," *Sherlock Holmes Journal,* Spring, 1961, 5, 50–52.

☞ Index

Index

of

Names and Topics

Index
of
Recipes